Kiera Clayton Travel Guide To

BAMBERG

GERMANY

Your Comprehensive Vacation Guide to Bamberg:
Unveiling Hidden Treasures

KIERA CLAYTON

COPYRIGHT NOTICE

DISCLAIMER

The information provided in this publication is intended for educational purposes only. It has been sourced from materials believed to be reliable at the time of publication. However, the opinions and information contained herein are subject to change without prior notice.

Readers acknowledge that the Author/Publisher is not offering legal, financial, or professional advice. The Publisher/Author makes no guarantees as to the accuracy, completeness, or adequacy of the information provided.

The Publisher assumes no responsibility for any errors, omissions, or misinterpretations of the information presented. The Publisher/Author expressly disclaims liability for any consequences arising from the use or application of the material contained in this book.

TABLE OF CONTENTS

INTRODUCTION

WELCOME TO BAMBERG

Welcome to Bamberg! Whether you're a history enthusiast, a foodie, a nature lover, or just looking for a relaxing vacation, Bamberg has something for everyone. Nestled in the heart of Bavaria, Germany, this lovely city is known for its well-preserved medieval architecture, rich cultural legacy, and energetic environment. Join me on a trip to discover Bamberg's hidden jewels and unique experiences.

As you walk through the cobblestone streets of Bamberg, you'll be transported back in time to a world where history comes alive at every turn. Every element of this UNESCO World Heritage Site, from the magnificent Bamberg Cathedral to the quaint half-timbered cottages surrounding the riverbanks, exudes charm and character. Whether you're strolling through the Old Town's meandering lanes or sipping a local brew in one of the old beer gardens, you'll be fascinated by Bamberg's timeless beauty and kind welcome.

About The Travel Guide

Welcome to your ideal partner for exploring Bamberg! This travel guide is intended to give you with all of the information you need to make the most of your trip to this wonderful city. Whether you're a first-time visitor or an experienced traveler, you'll find insider information, recommended activities, food options, lodging recommendations, and more to help you make amazing memories in Bamberg.

Why Bamberg?

You might be asking why you should consider Bamberg as your next travel location. So, let me explain why Bamberg is a must-see city:

Historical Charm: Bamberg's Old Town is a UNESCO World Heritage Site, with over 1,000 years of history and architecture that have been magnificently maintained. From medieval cathedrals to Baroque castles, every part of Bamberg is rich in history and culture.

Culinary Delights: Food lovers rejoice! Bamberg is well-known for its traditional Bavarian food, which includes substantial sausages, flavorful schnitzels, and, of course, its world-class beer. Don't pass up the opportunity to experience local specialties at one of Bamberg's numerous breweries, beer gardens, and quaint taverns.

Natural Beauty: Surrounded by rolling hills, luscious vineyards, and quiet rivers, Bamberg provides ample possibilities for outdoor enthusiasts to explore the great outside. Whether you're trekking the picturesque paths of the Franconian countryside or boating down the Main-Danube Canal, Bamberg's natural splendor will fascinate you.

Cultural Legacy: Bamberg is a cultural hub that proudly cherishes its legacy, with a thriving arts scene, vivid festivals, and bustling markets. From classical concerts at the Concert Hall to traditional folk festivals such as Sandkerwa, there is always something spectacular going on in Bamberg.

Warm Hospitality: Finally, Bamberg is well-known for its welcoming residents and genuine welcome. Whether you're conversing with a brewer in a beer garden or a shopkeeper in the market square, you'll be greeted warmly and treated like family in Bamberg.

How To Use This Guide

Navigating a new city can be stressful, but don't worry! This guide will help you every step of the way. Here's how to make the best of it:

Explore The Chapters: This book is separated into chapters, each of which focuses on a different area of Bamberg, such as attractions and restaurants, practical recommendations, and cultural experiences. Take your time exploring each chapter and seeing what Bamberg has to offer.

Use The Subheadings: Each chapter contains subheadings that divide the content into more specific areas. Whether you're looking for lodging recommendations, transportation choices, or insider advice, the subheadings will help you get what you need.

Take Notes And Bookmarks: Feel free to take notes or bookmark your favorite areas for future reference during your vacation. Whether you're organizing your schedule or looking for instructions on the go, having this guide on hand will make your trip to Bamberg go smoothly and enjoyable.

Get Inspired: Finally, let this guide motivate you to explore Bamberg beyond the tourist highlights. While the must-see attractions are undoubtedly worth seeing, don't be afraid to venture off the beaten path and uncover hidden jewels and local treasures that will make your trip truly unforgettable.

With this book in hand, you're ready to go on an excursion to Bamberg and discover all that this wonderful city has to offer. So pack your luggage, lace up your walking shoes, and prepare for an incredible tour into the heart of Bavaria!

Are you intrigued by Bamberg's historical charm, gastronomic pleasures, and friendly hospitality? Allow this book to be your passport to discovering this magical city and making memories that will last a lifetime. Prepare to be immersed in the magic of Bamberg, where every cobblestone street tells a story and every corner invites you to find something new.

CHAPTER 1

INTRODUCTION TO BAMBERG

Bamberg, located in the heart of Bavaria, Germany, captivates visitors with its medieval beauty, rich history, and scenic surroundings. In this chapter, we will look at the essence of Bamberg, including its history, geography, climate, and cultural significance.

Overview Of Bamberg

Bamberg, sometimes known as "Franconian Rome" or the "City of Seven Hills," is a UNESCO World Heritage Site renowned for its well-preserved medieval architecture, quaint cobblestone lanes, and picturesque position along the Regnitz River. Bamberg, founded in the tenth century, has a distinct blend of Romanesque, Gothic, and Baroque elements, making it a favorite among history buffs and architecture enthusiasts.

The city is organized into three major districts: Old Town (Altstadt), Island District (Inselstadt), and Hill District (Bergstadt). Each neighborhood has its own particular personality and attractions, ranging from the renowned Bamberg Cathedral and the lovely Little Venice to the ancient Altenburg Castle and the attractive half-timbered homes.

Bamberg is especially known for its beer culture, with nine breweries making traditional Franconian beers like as the well-known Rauchbier (smoked beer). The city's beer gardens, bars, and breweries allow tourists to enjoy these local beers in classic Bavarian settings.

Brief History Of Bamberg

Bamberg's history extends back over a thousand years to Emperor Henry II's reign, when the city was built in 1007. Under his administration, Bamberg thrived as a center of ecclesiastical and political power, giving it the nickname "Rome of Franconia." The city's strategic location at the crossroads of vital trade routes added to its prosperity, bringing merchants, artisans, and intellectuals from all over.

In the centuries that followed, Bamberg expanded and prospered, becoming an important ecclesiastical city and the seat of the powerful Bamberg bishopric. During the Middle Ages and Renaissance periods, prominent landmarks such as Bamberg Cathedral, Altenburg Castle, and the Old Town Hall were built, which added to the city's status and cultural significance.

Despite being damaged during World War II, Bamberg surprisingly avoided the widespread destruction that struck many other German cities, thanks to the efforts of local inhabitants and Allied soldiers to preserve its ancient heritage. Bamberg was named a UNESCO World Heritage Site in 1993 for its outstanding architectural and cultural importance, guaranteeing that future generations can appreciate its legacy.

Geography And Climate

Bamberg, located in the Upper Franconia area of Bavaria, has a gorgeous location surrounded by rolling hills, green valleys, and the peaceful waters of the Regnitz and Main rivers. The city's landscape is defined by its seven hills, which offer breathtaking panoramic views of the surrounding countryside and city below.

Bamberg has a temperate marine climate, with warm summers, chilly winters, and moderate rainfall all year. Summers are normally mild and pleasant, with temperatures averaging 20-25°C (68-77°F), while winters are chilly but rarely severe, with temperatures ranging from 0-5°C (32-41°F). The greatest season to visit Bamberg is in the spring and summer, when the weather is pleasant and the city is bustling with outdoor festivals, markets, and cultural events.

Cultural Significance

Bamberg's cultural significance goes far beyond its architectural beauty and historical sites. The city is a thriving center of arts, music, theater, and culinary traditions, drawing visitors from all over the world to enjoy its distinct cultural history.

One of Bamberg's most treasured cultural traditions is its UNESCO-designated Christmas Market, which transforms the city into a winter paradise during the holidays. The Christmas Market provides a spectacular experience for visitors of all ages, with festive decorations and glittering lights among traditional crafts and seasonal delights.

Bamberg is also well-known for its classical music culture, which boasts a long history of composers, players, and orchestras that continue to thrive today. The yearly Bamberg Symphony Orchestra concerts, which take place in venues such as the Konzerthalle Bamberg and the Bamberg Cathedral, draw music enthusiasts from all over the world.

Furthermore, Bamberg's culinary culture reflects the city's gastronomic legacy, with a variety of traditional Bavarian diners, gourmet restaurants, and bustling markets serving real Franconian cuisine. From substantial sausages and pretzels to flavorful schnitzels and regional cheeses, Bamberg's culinary offerings will excite your taste buds and leave you wanting more.

To summarize, Bamberg's cultural significance stems not only from its historic landmarks and architectural marvels, but also from its thriving artistic scene, musical history, and culinary traditions. Whether you're strolling through the city's ancient alleyways, attending a classical symphony, or eating local specialties in a beer garden, Bamberg has a rich tapestry of cultural experiences waiting to be found.

This chapter provides an overview of Bamberg, including its history, topography, climate, and cultural significance. As you continue reading this travel guide, you'll learn more about this wonderful city and everything it has to offer. So, let us delve deeper into the beauties of Bamberg and go on a memorable journey together!

CHAPTER 2

GETTING TO BAMBERG

Bamberg, located in the heart of Bavaria, Germany, invites visitors from all over the world with its medieval beauty, rich history, and beautiful surroundings. In this chapter, we'll look at the different ways to get to Bamberg, such as flying, taking a train, and driving.

Transportation Options

When planning your trip to Bamberg, you'll have several transportation options to consider, depending on your preferences, budget, and travel itinerary. Here are some of the most popular ways to reach Bamberg:

Air Travel: Bamberg's nearest international airport is Nuremberg Airport (NUE), which is around 60 kilometers south of town. From Nuremberg Airport, you can take a direct train or bus to Bamberg, which takes 45 minutes to an hour. Alternatively, you can fly into Munich Airport (MUC) or Frankfurt Airport (FRA), both of which have substantial flight connections and are located roughly 200-250 kilometers from Bamberg. To get to Bamberg from Munich or Frankfurt Airport, use the train or rent a car.

Train Services: Bamberg is well-connected to Germany's large railway network, with Deutsche Bahn (DB) operating frequent train services to the city's major train station, Bamberg Hauptbahnhof. High-speed ICE trains, regional express (RE) trains, and regionalbahn (RB) trains allow easy access to large cities like Munich, Frankfurt, Nuremberg, and Berlin, as well as smaller towns and villages around the region. The rail ride from Nuremberg to Bamberg usually takes 30-45 minutes, however trips from Munich or Frankfurt can take 2-3 hours, depending on the route and service.

Bus Services: Several long-distance bus companies provide service to Bamberg from major cities around Germany and Europe. FlixBus, MeinFernbus, and Eurolines are among the most popular bus companies that provide affordable and comfortable coach transportation to Bamberg. The major bus terminal in Bamberg lies near the train station, allowing easy access to the city center and neighboring areas.

Car Rental: For travelers who prefer the flexibility and freedom of driving, renting a car is a convenient way to reach Bamberg. Europcar, Hertz, and Sixt have offices at Nuremberg Airport and other major German airports where you can pick up your rental car upon arrival. Bamberg is easily accessible from the airport by the A73 road, which takes around 45-60 minutes to drive, depending on traffic.

Airports And Railway Stations

Nuremberg Airport (NUE): Nuremberg Airport, located around 60 kilometers south of Bamberg, is the region's nearest international airport. The airport provides direct flights to and from major European destinations like London, Paris, Amsterdam, and Zurich, as well as domestic flights to Berlin, Munich, and Hamburg. Deutsche Bahn operates frequent direct train services from the airport to Bamberg.

Bamberg Hauptbahnhof (Major Train Station): Bamberg Hauptbahnhof is the city's major railway station, situated in the heart of the Old Town. The station serves as a significant center for regional and long-distance train services, connecting cities throughout Germany and Europe. High-speed ICE trains, regional express (RE) trains, and regionalbahn (RB) trains all stop at Bamberg Hauptbahnhof, giving you quick access to the city center and surrounding areas.

Driving Directions And Parking

If you're driving to Bamberg, here are some routes and parking options to assist you get there:

From Nuremberg Airport: From Nuremberg Airport, take the A3 towards Würzburg, then merge onto the A73 towards Bamberg. Follow the signs to Bamberg until you reach your destination. Bamberg has street parking, public parking facilities, and reserved parking places near major attractions and sites. Before leaving your vehicle, make sure to verify the parking restrictions and taxes.

From Munich Airport (MUC): From Munich Airport, take the A9 towards Nuremberg, then merge onto the A73 towards Bamberg. Follow the signs to Bamberg until you reach your destination. Alternatively, take the A92 motorway to

Landshut, then the A93 motorway to Regensburg, where you may connect to the A3 motorway to Nuremberg and carry on to Bamberg.

From Frankfurt Airport (FRA): From Frankfurt Airport, take the A3 towards Würzburg, then merge onto the A73 towards Bamberg. Follow the signs to Bamberg until you reach your destination. Alternatively, you can take the A5 towards Heidelberg and then the A6 towards Nuremberg, where you can connect with the A73 towards Bamberg.

When you arrive in Bamberg, you'll have numerous parking alternatives, including on-street parking, public parking garages, and designated parking lots near major sites and monuments. To avoid fines or penalties, comply with local parking rules, such as time limitations and payment requirements.

We looked at the several modes of transportation accessible for getting to Bamberg, such as air travel, train services, and driving directions. Whether you choose to fly, take the train, or drive, there are easy and effective methods to get to this picturesque city in the heart of Bavaria. Bamberg is easily accessible via international airports, large train stations, well-maintained highways, and beautiful routes.

This chapter tries to make it easier for passengers to organize their trip to Bamberg by offering thorough information on transportation options, airports, train stations, and driving directions. Whether you're arriving from a neighboring city or a distant country, you'll find all the information you need to get to your destination quickly.

As you plan your trip to Bamberg, bear in mind that the city's central location, good transportation infrastructure, and convenient parking facilities make it an ideal base for visiting the surrounding area. Whether you're traveling alone, with family or friends, or on a romantic trip, Bamberg welcomes you with open arms and promises an amazing experience full of history, culture, and charm.

Whether you are coming for business or pleasure, arranging your trip to Bamberg is an exciting aspect of the journey. With its rich history, gorgeous architecture, and dynamic cultural scene, Bamberg has something for everyone, from history buffs and foodies to outdoor adventurers and art fans. So pack your luggage, reserve your tickets, and prepare to go on an unforgettable journey to Bamberg, where every cobblestone street tells a story and every bend offers a new discovery.

This chapter contains detailed information on how to travel to Bamberg, including transit choices, airports, train stations, driving directions, and parking. We hope that by providing practical recommendations and detailed information, guests will be able to plan their trip to Bamberg with confidence. Whether you arrive by flight, rail, or vehicle, getting to Bamberg is a smooth process that allows you to focus on discovering everything this wonderful city has to offer. So sit back, relax, and enjoy the ride as you head to Bamberg, where adventure lies around every corner.

CHAPTER 3

ACCOMMOATIONS IN BAMBERG

Bamberg, a city rich in history and culture, has a wide range of hotel alternatives to fit every traveler's needs and interests. In this chapter, we'll look at a variety of Bamberg lodging options, including opulent resorts, quaint guesthouses, and budget-friendly hotels.

Overview Of Accommodation Options

Travelers in Bamberg have a plethora of options for finding the ideal location to stay. From historic hotels and boutique guesthouses to modern apartments and low-cost hostels, there is something for everyone's taste and budget. Here's a summary of the various sorts of accommodations available in Bamberg:

Hotels: Bamberg has a diverse range of hotels, from opulent 5-star resorts to quaint boutique hotels and family-run places. Many hotels are in the city center, within walking distance of main attractions, restaurants, and retail malls.

Guesthouses And Bed And Breakfasts: If you want a more private and personalized experience, stay in a Bamberg guesthouse or bed & breakfast. These charming motels frequently include home-cooked breakfasts, friendly hosts, and distinctive decor that reflects the city's history.

Apartments And Vacation Rentals: If you prefer the freedom and convenience of self-catering accommodations, Bamberg offers a wide range of apartments and vacation rentals. Whether you're traveling alone, with family, or in a group, renting an apartment allows you to explore the city like a native while enjoying the comforts of home away from home.

Hostels And Budget Hotels: Budget-conscious travelers will appreciate Bamberg's economical accommodation options, which include hostels, budget hotels, and guesthouses. These accommodations have modest amenities, pleasant rooms, and shared facilities, making them perfect for backpackers, students, and budget-conscious guests.

Luxury Resorts: Bamberg has a number of beautiful resorts and spa hotels for people looking for a relaxing vacation. These upmarket properties, nestled among lush gardens, gorgeous vistas, and serene environs, provide deluxe facilities, gourmet dining, and world-class service for an exceptional visit.

No matter where you choose to stay in Bamberg, you will undoubtedly discover lodgings that match your needs and improve your visit to this wonderful city.

Luxury Resorts

For guests seeking the best in comfort, luxury, and relaxation, Bamberg has a range of superb resorts and spa hotels that promise a genuinely luxurious experience. Here are some of the best luxury resorts in Bamberg:

Welcome Hotel Residenzschloss Bamberg: Located in the heart of Bamberg's Old Town, the Welcome Hotel Residenzschloss Bamberg is a magnificent getaway located in a medieval castle. This 5-star hotel exudes richness and elegance with beautiful rooms and suites furnished in period style, marble bathrooms, and modern conveniences. Guests can relax in the hotel's spa and wellness center, which features a variety of rejuvenating treatments, saunas, and an indoor swimming pool. The hotel's gourmet restaurant delivers exceptional cuisine made with locally produced ingredients, while the contemporary bar serves a variety of great wine and cocktails.

Brose Arena Hotel Bamberg: Adjacent to Bamberg's top sports and event arena, the Brose Arena Hotel Bamberg provides contemporary luxury and convenience in the city center. The hotel's spacious rooms and suites have modern décor, soft linen, and cutting-edge facilities, ensuring that visitors have a comfortable and relaxing stay. The hotel's spa section features a sauna, steam bath, and fitness center, and the rooftop terrace provides panoramic views of the Bamberg skyline. Guests can enjoy great dining at the hotel's restaurant, which specializes in regional and international dishes, or unwind with a drink at the trendy bar.

Burg Rabenstein: Burg Rabenstein is a medieval castle hotel surrounded by magnificent woodlands and meadows, only a short drive from Bamberg. This lovely hotel, which dates back to the 12th century, provides magnificent lodgings in a fairy-tale setting, with elegantly decorated rooms and suites boasting antique furnishings, canopy beds, and breathtaking vistas. Guests can indulge in gourmet dining in the hotel's restaurant, which serves delicious dishes inspired by traditional Franconian cuisine, or relax with a glass of wine by the fireplace in the pleasant lounge. The hotel also provides a variety of outdoor activities such as hiking, horseback riding, and falconry exhibitions, making it an excellent choice for both nature enthusiasts and adventure seekers.

Schloss Burgellern: Schloss Burgellern is a lovely castle hotel located just outside of Bamberg, surrounded by wonderfully planted gardens and vineyards. The hotel's beautiful rooms and suites are individually designed in a traditional style, complete with antique furnishings, four-poster mattresses, and contemporary facilities. Guests can unwind at the hotel's spa and wellness center, which includes a sauna, steam bath, and massage treatments, or explore the local countryside by foot or bicycle. The hotel's gourmet restaurant serves seasonal cuisine made with locally sourced ingredients, and the patio has spectacular views of the surrounding countryside. Schloss Burgellern's calm setting and old-world elegance make it the ideal refuge for couples looking for a romantic holiday or those hoping to unwind in a peaceful environment.

Hotel Nepomuk: Located on the banks of the Regnitz River in Bamberg's charming Old Town, Hotel Nepomuk combines contemporary luxury with a historic setting. The hotel's elegant rooms and suites have a sleek style, modern conveniences, and breathtaking views of the river or cityscape. Guests can enjoy a variety of wellness amenities, such as a sauna and fitness center, or unwind with a drink on the rooftop terrace overlooking the river. The hotel's restaurant offers unique cuisine influenced by Bavarian and foreign flavors, with a focus on fresh, locally produced ingredients.

Best Western Hotel Bamberg: The Best Western Hotel Bamberg, conveniently located near Bamberg's major train station, provides modern comfort and convenience for visitors to the city. The hotel's large rooms and suites are elegantly appointed and come with all the amenities you need for a comfortable stay, such as free Wi-Fi, flat-screen TVs, and coffee/tea makers. Guests can begin the day with a delicious breakfast buffet offered in the hotel's bright and spacious dining area, or relax with a drink at the pleasant hotel bar. With its convenient location and helpful staff, the Best Western Hotel Bamberg is a popular choice for both business and leisure tourists.

These are only a few of Bamberg's finest resorts and spa hotels. Whether you're celebrating a special occasion, looking for a romantic retreat, or simply looking for a relaxing vacation, these accommodations provide the ideal balance of comfort, elegance, and refinement for an exceptional stay in Bamberg.

In conclusion, Bamberg's luxury resorts offer discerning tourists a variety of upmarket rooms, world-class amenities, and personalized service in a picturesque and historic location. Whether you stay in a castle hotel, riverside retreat, or boutique property, you'll be treated to the ultimate in luxury and leisure throughout your vacation to Bamberg.

In this chapter, we looked at the luxury resorts and spa hotels in Bamberg, Germany, that cater to discerning guests seeking an exquisite experience. From medieval castle hotels to modern riverfront retreats, these properties offer the ideal balance of comfort, elegance, and refinement for a memorable visit in this attractive city. Whether you want a romantic holiday, a soothing retreat, or just a taste of luxury, Bamberg's luxury resorts offers something for everyone. So, why wait? Book a stay at one of these beautiful homes and enjoy the pinnacle of luxury in Bamberg!

Budget-Friendly Hotels

Travelers looking for low-cost accommodations in Bamberg will find a range of hotels with pleasant rooms, handy amenities, and reasonable rates. Here are some alternatives for affordable hotels in Bamberg:

Ibis Budget Bamberg: Located near Bamberg's major train station, the Ibis Budget Bamberg provides clean and comfortable rooms at affordable prices. The hotel's modern rooms include a simple style, comfortable linen, and necessary facilities like free Wi-Fi and flat-screen TVs. Every morning, guests can enjoy a complimentary breakfast buffet and make use of the hotel's 24-hour front desk and on-site parking.

Bamberg Inn: Located in a quiet residential neighborhood within a short walk from the city center, Bamberg Inn provides economical lodging in a cozy guesthouse atmosphere. The hotel's plain yet comfortable rooms provide with basic conveniences including private bathrooms, flat-screen TVs, and complimentary Wi-Fi. Guests can relax in the hotel's garden courtyard or visit the neighboring sights and historic buildings in Bamberg.

Hotel Garni Altenburgblick: Located on the outskirts of Bamberg's Old Town, Hotel garni Altenburgblick provides affordable lodgings with stunning views of the Altenburg Castle. The hotel's spacious rooms have traditional Bavarian décor, comfy furnishings, and modern facilities like satellite TV and free Wi-Fi. Guests can begin their day with a delicious breakfast buffet offered in the hotel's dining room, followed by easy access to the city center by public transportation or a leisurely stroll along the river.

Hotel Europa Bamberg: Located within walking distance of Bamberg's main attractions, Hotel Europa Bamberg provides economical lodging in a convenient setting. The hotel's modest yet trendy rooms come with modern amenities including flat-screen TVs, minibars, and free Wi-Fi. Every morning, guests may enjoy a complimentary breakfast buffet and make use of the hotel's on-site parking and bicycle rental amenities.

Hotel Andres: Located in a historic building in Bamberg's Old Town, Hotel Andres provides affordable lodgings with a touch of charm and character. The hotel's charming rooms include traditional hardwood furnishings, comfy bedding, and modern amenities like satellite TV and free Wi-Fi. Guests can relax in the hotel's courtyard garden or visit neighboring sites like the Bamberg Cathedral and the Old Town Hall.

These are just a few examples of Bamberg's budget-friendly hotels that provide comfortable and convenient accommodations. Whether you're on a tight budget, planning a quick trip, or simply trying to save money on lodging, these hotels offer a comfortable and handy base for seeing everything Bamberg has to offer.

Boutique Guesthouses

For those looking for a more private and customized experience, Bamberg has a variety of boutique guesthouses that mix charm, character, and hospitality in distinctive and inviting surroundings. Here are some choices for boutique guesthouses in Bamberg:

Villa Geyersworth: Located on the banks of the Regnitz River, Villa Geyersworth is a delightful boutique hotel located in a historic villa from the nineteenth century. The guesthouse has attractively designed rooms and suites with fashionable decor, comfortable furnishings, and modern facilities like flat-screen TVs, minibars, and complimentary

Wi-Fi. Guests can enjoy a gourmet breakfast in the hotel's exquisite dining room or unwind in the tranquil courtyard garden overlooking the river.

Hotel Wohnbar: Hotel Wohnbar is a boutique guesthouse in Bamberg's Old Town that blends contemporary design with historical charm. The hotel's rooms are individually furnished with unique furnishings, artistic elements, and modern facilities such as flat-screen TVs, minibars, and complimentary Wi-Fi. Guests can unwind in the hotel's quiet lounge area or have a drink at the modern bar, which offers a variety of exquisite wines and cocktails.

Altstadt-Hotel Molitor: Located in a historic building in Bamberg's Old Town, is a boutique guesthouse that provides warm lodgings with a personal touch. The hotel's lovely rooms are furnished in traditional Bavarian style, with oak furnishings, plush bedding, and modern facilities like flat-screen TVs and free Wi-Fi. Guests can begin their day with a complimentary breakfast buffet offered in the hotel's charming dining area before exploring the neighboring sites and landmarks of Bamberg on foot.

Boutique-Hotel Villa Katharina: Located in a restored medieval villa near Bamberg's city center, this boutique hotel offers attractive decor and modern services. The hotel's spacious rooms and suites have luxurious bedding, hardwood flooring, and stunning views of the surrounding gardens and countryside. Guests can relax in the hotel's spa area, which contains a sauna and steam room, or sip a glass of wine on the terrace that overlooks the lovely environment.

Gästehaus Kachelofen: Located in the heart of Bamberg's Old Town, Gästehaus Kachelofen is a pleasant boutique guesthouse built in a historic building from the 17th century. The guesthouse has comfortable lodgings with a rustic character, including exposed wooden beams, antique furnishings, and modern facilities like flat-screen TVs and complimentary Wi-Fi. Guests can enjoy a complimentary breakfast in the hotel's lovely breakfast room or unwind in the pleasant courtyard garden.

These are just a few examples of Bamberg boutique guesthouses that provide guests with a one-of-a-kind and unforgettable experience in a private and warm environment. Whether you're looking for historic charm, contemporary design, or breathtaking vistas, these boutique accommodations provide for an unforgettable visit in Bamberg.

In this chapter, we've looked at the many types of accommodations accessible in Bamberg, such as budget-friendly hotels and boutique guest homes. From quiet guesthouses with historic charm to inexpensive hotels with modern conveniences, tourists will find the ideal place to stay in Bamberg based on their preferences and budget. Whether you're looking for affordable accommodations or boutique luxury, Bamberg has something for everyone, assuring a comfortable and entertaining stay in this lovely city.

Unique Stays

For guests seeking a genuinely unforgettable and one-of-a-kind experience, Bamberg has a variety of unique lodgings that go beyond typical hotels and guesthouses. These one-of-a-kind accommodations in Bamberg include historic castles and medieval towers, as well as charming boat lodges and rustic farm stays. Here are some alternatives for interesting accommodations in Bamberg:

Schloss Seehof: Just outside of Bamberg, Schloss Seehof is a magnificent baroque palace surrounded by gorgeous gardens and a quiet lake. This historic landmark provides luxurious accommodations in attractively decorated rooms and suites outfitted with antique furnishings, plush linen, and contemporary comforts. Guests can explore the royal grounds, which include groomed gardens, elegant fountains, and gorgeous walking trails, as well as engage in leisure activities such as fishing, boating, and lakeside picnics. Schloss Seehof, with its regal ambiance and magnificent surroundings, offers a truly unique stay in Bamberg.

Altes Rathaus (Old Town Hall): Perched on a bridge across the Regnitz River, is one of Bamberg's most distinctive buildings and a one-of-a-kind location to stay. The old structure is a nice guesthouse with comfortable rooms that overlook the river and the city's picturesque skyline. Guests can experience the building's rich history and architectural elegance while staying in the center of Bamberg's Old Town, close to the city's major attractions, restaurants, and retail areas. Staying at the Altes Rathaus provides a unique opportunity to experience Bamberg's legacy firsthand and immerse yourself in the city's dynamic environment.

Floating Homes on the Regnitz River: Staying in one of Bamberg's floating homes on the Regnitz River is a genuinely unique and wonderful experience. These beautiful houseboats provide snug rooms with breathtaking views of the river and the city's historical sites. Guests can unwind on the deck, eat outside, or simply watch the world go by as they cruise down the serene waters of the Regnitz. Floating homes, with their quiet ambiance and gorgeous surroundings, offer a peaceful and unforgettable stay in Bamberg.

Bauernhof (Farm Stays): For tourists looking for a rustic and immersive experience, consider staying in a Bauernhof, or traditional farm stay, in the Bavarian countryside near Bamberg. These family-run farms provide comfortable lodging in beautiful guesthouses or holiday flats, surrounded by lush meadows, rolling hills, and lovely villages. Guests can take part in agricultural chores including milking cows, feeding animals, harvesting crops, or simply relaxing in the tranquil countryside. Bauernhof stays offer a one-of-a-kind opportunity to experience rural living in Bavaria while also connecting with nature.

Medieval Tower Apartments: For a genuinely unique and historic experience, consider staying in one of Bamberg's medieval tower apartments. These historical towers have been meticulously repaired and transformed into modern rooms, with panoramic views of the city skyline and historic monuments. Guests can ascend the spiral staircases, observe the original stone walls and wooden beams, and learn about Bamberg's rich history and architectural legacy. Staying in a medieval tower apartment provides a once-in-a-lifetime opportunity to explore the city's medieval past while enjoying modern comforts and amenities.

These are just a few examples of distinctive Bamberg hotels that provide guests with an unforgettable experience in this attractive city. Whether you're looking for historic charm, scenic beauty, or immersive experiences, these one-of-a-kind hotels set the tone for an unforgettable visit in Bamberg.

Top Recommended Accommodations

Selecting the appropriate lodging is critical for a memorable and enjoyable stay in Bamberg. To assist you in finding the ideal place to stay, here are some of the top suggested lodgings in Bamberg based on traveler reviews, amenities, and location:

Hotel Villa Geyersworth: Set in a historic villa on the banks of the Regnitz River, Hotel Villa Geyersworth provides magnificent accommodations with breathtaking views of the river and the city's Old Town. The hotel's spacious rooms and suites have luxury furniture, modern conveniences, and personalized service to ensure that visitors have a pleasant and enjoyable stay. The hotel's gourmet restaurant delivers delectable regional cuisine cooked with fresh, locally produced ingredients, and the terrace provides a gorgeous backdrop for outdoor dining.

Altstadthotel Molitor: Located in the heart of Bamberg's Old Town, Altstadthotel Molitor is a beautiful boutique hotel housed in a historic structure from the 17th century. The hotel's spacious rooms are individually designed with old furnishings and modern facilities, making it a warm and appealing place for guests. The hotel's breakfast buffet includes a variety of delectable local specialties such as freshly baked bread, pastries, and homemade jams, while the quiet lounge provides a relaxing environment to unwind with a book or a drink.

Hotel Nepomuk: Located on the banks of the Regnitz River, Hotel Nepomuk combines contemporary luxury with a historic setting. The hotel's elegant rooms and suites include modern design, comfy furnishings, and stunning views of the river or cityscape. Guests can take advantage of a variety of services, including a spa center with sauna and steam room, a rooftop terrace with panoramic views, and a gourmet restaurant providing inventive cuisine prepared with seasonal ingredients.

Welcome Hotel Residenzschloss Bamberg: Housed within a medieval castle in Bamberg's Old Town, this hotel provides elegant accommodations with a touch of regal elegance. The hotel's spacious rooms and suites are artistically designed with antique antiques, plush bedding, and modern facilities, ensuring that guests have a relaxing and luxurious stay. The hotel's spa and wellness center provide a variety of treatments and amenities, including a sauna, steam bath, and indoor swimming pool, while the gourmet restaurant delivers delectable cuisine influenced by the region's culinary culture.

Hotel Alt-Ringlein: Located in a historic building overlooking the lovely Little Venice district, Hotel Alt-Ringlein provides comfortable lodgings with authentic Bavarian charm. The hotel's rustic rooms have wooden furnishings, comfy bedding, and modern facilities, creating a warm and welcoming ambiance for guests. The hotel's restaurant serves great Franconian dishes and local beers, while the terrace provides panoramic views of the river and the city's distinctive cityscape.

These are just a handful of the top rated accommodations in Bamberg, ensuring that visitors have a comfortable, convenient, and memorable stay in this charming city. Whether you're looking for luxury, historic charm, or scenic beauty, these hotels are the ideal base for discovering everything Bamberg has to offer.

Choosing The Right Accommodation For You

Choosing the appropriate accommodations is an important aspect of arranging a successful trip to Bamberg. Finding the ideal place to stay can improve your overall trip experience, with options ranging from luxury hotels to intimate guesthouses and one-of-a-kind stays. When choosing the perfect hotel for you in Bamberg, consider the following factors:

Location: Consider the location of your accommodation in proximity to the sights and activities you intend to do in Bamberg. Staying near the city center gives you easy access to key landmarks, restaurants, and shopping districts, whilst accommodations on the outskirts provide a quieter ambiance and may be more ideal for tourists looking for a peaceful getaway.

Budget: Determine your lodging budget and look for possibilities that fit inside it. Bamberg has a wide range of accommodations to suit any budget, from luxury resorts to budget-friendly hotels and guesthouses. Remember that costs might fluctuate based on the season, so book ahead of time to get the best deals.

Amenities: Consider the services and facilities provided by the accommodation, such as Wi-Fi, breakfast, parking, and recreational opportunities. Determine which amenities are necessary for your stay and select rooms that fit your requirements and preferences.

Reviews And Ratings: Read previous guests' reviews and ratings to get a sense of the accommodation's quality and service. Websites like TripAdvisor, Booking.com, and Google Reviews provide useful information and opinions from previous guests.

Unique Features: Accommodations with particular features or amenities, such as historic charm, beautiful views, or themed rooms, can provide a one-of-a-kind and unforgettable experience. Boutique hotels, castle stays, and floating houses provide unique experiences that add excitement to your vacation.

Traveling With Pets Or Family: If you're traveling with dogs or family members, look for lodgings that are pet-friendly or include family-friendly features like connecting rooms, cribs, and daycare services. Before booking, confirm the accommodation's policies, as well as any additional costs or restrictions.

By taking these criteria into account and conducting comprehensive research, you may find the ideal lodging to fit your needs, tastes, and budget, ensuring a comfortable and pleasurable stay in Bamberg.

Booking Tips And Tricks

Booking accommodations in Bamberg may be a simple procedure if you follow these tips and methods for getting the greatest discounts and having a pleasant reservation experience:

Book In Advance: To get the greatest pricing and availability, book your accommodations well in advance, especially if you're visiting during busy seasons like summer or major events and festivals. Booking early gives you more options and prevents last-minute stress.

Compare Rates: Use online booking platforms and travel websites to compare the rates, facilities, and reviews of various Bamberg lodgings. Booking.com, Expedia, and Hotels.com allow you to easily compare rates and book directly with the hotel or through third-party suppliers.

Sign Up for Alerts and Deals: Subscribe to email newsletters and alerts from booking companies to stay up to date on special offers, discounts, and promotions for Bamberg accommodations. Many booking systems provide subscribers with unique bargains and member-only discounts, allowing them to save money on their stay.

Flexible Dates And Times: If your trip dates are flexible, you may consider changing your schedule to take advantage of lower rates and more availability. Staying at off-peak hours or midweek can typically result in lower prices and less congested hotels.

Use Reward Programs: If you belong to a hotel loyalty or travel rewards program, use your points or miles to book rooms in Bamberg. Many hotel businesses and booking sites reward loyal customers with free nights, room upgrades, and special bonuses.

Read The Fine Print: Before making a reservation, carefully review the terms and conditions, cancellation policies, and any additional costs or restrictions. Pay attention to the cancellation policy, as certain lodgings may impose a fee for cancellations made within a specific timeframe.

Contact The Accommodation Directly: If you have any specific preferences or requirements for your stay, such as room preferences, dietary restrictions, or special requests, you should contact the accommodation directly to discuss them. Hotel staff are frequently willing to meet unique requests and offer individual help to guarantee a great visit.

By following these booking tips and methods, you may get the best rates, select the ideal hotel, and have a stress-free reservation experience for your trip to Bamberg.

In this chapter, we've discussed how to find the best hotel for your stay in Bamberg, as well as tips and tactics for reserving rooms efficiently. Whether you want elegance, affordability, or one-of-a-kind experiences, Bamberg has something for everyone's needs and interests. With careful planning and study, you can locate the ideal place to stay and have a relaxing and memorable visit to this picturesque city in Bavaria.

CHAPTER 4

EXPLORING BAMBERG'S OLD TOWN

Bamberg's Old Town is a treasure mine of historical, cultural, and architectural splendor. This medieval city, a UNESCO World Heritage Site since 1993, has a rich tapestry of historical relics, architectural marvels, and lovely cobblestone lanes. In this chapter, we'll take a closer look at what awaits you when you explore Bamberg's Old Town.

UNESCO World Heritage Site

Bamberg's Old Town is a UNESCO World Heritage Site, designated for its exceptional universal value and cultural importance. The city's well-preserved medieval layout, gorgeous architecture, and rich history make it a must-see destination for those looking to immerse themselves in the past. Bamberg's Old Town, with its stately churches and historic bridges, as well as its picturesque squares and winding alleyways, embodies centuries of Bavarian heritage and tradition.

Altstadt Or Old Town: The core of Bamberg's UNESCO World Heritage Site is its Altstadt, or Old Town, a maze of narrow streets and alleyways adorned with colorful half-timbered houses, medieval churches, and historic structures. As you walk along the cobblestone streets, you'll be transported back in time to the Middle Ages, surrounded by sights and sounds from a bygone age.

Bamberg Cathedral: The Bamberg Cathedral, also known as the Imperial Cathedral of St. Peter and St. George, is a feature of the UNESCO World Heritage Site in Bamberg. This splendid Romanesque cathedral, constructed in the 11th century, is a masterpiece of medieval architecture and houses the tombs of Emperor Henry II and his wife, Empress Cunigunde. Visitors visiting Bamberg should not miss the Bamberg Cathedral, which has soaring spires, beautiful sculptures, and an awe-inspiring interior.

Altes Rathaus: This is another architectural jewel in Bamberg's Old Town is the Altes Rathaus, or Old Town Hall, a remarkable structure located on a bridge above the Regnitz River. The Altes Rathaus, which dates back to the 14th century, is one of Bamberg's most recognizable structures and represents the city's rich history and legacy. Visitors can view the building's gorgeous front, which is covered with bright murals and ornate carvings, as well as explore its interior, which has an intriguing collection of historical objects and artwork.

In addition to its architectural marvels, Bamberg's Old Town has a thriving cultural environment, with museums, galleries, and theaters displaying the city's diverse artistic legacy. There are plenty of cultural sites to visit in Bamberg's UNESCO World Heritage Site, including the Bamberg State Library and Historical Museum, the E.T.A. Hoffmann Theater, and the Bamberg Symphony Orchestra.

Whether you're admiring the stately churches, meandering through the twisting alleyways, or taking in the ambiance in one of the city's attractive squares, Bamberg's Old Town will captivate your imagination and leave you with memories to last a lifetime.

Historic Landmarks

Bamberg's Old Town is home to numerous historical landmarks that provide insights into the city's long and fascinating history. From medieval churches and old defenses to historic bridges and palaces, these landmarks offer an intriguing view into Bamberg's architectural and cultural history.

Altes Rathaus: The Altes Rathaus, or Old Town Hall, is a stunning edifice located on a bridge over the Regnitz River and one of the most prominent buildings in Bamberg's Old Town. The Altes Rathaus, constructed in the 14th century, is a masterpiece of medieval architecture and a symbol of the city's civic pride. Its magnificent front, embellished with vivid frescoes and elaborate sculptures, makes it a famous tourist destination in Bamberg.

Bamberg Cathedral: Another must-see attraction in Bamberg is the Bamberg Cathedral, commonly known as the Imperial Cathedral of St. Peter and St. George. This magnificent Romanesque cathedral, erected in the eleventh century, is one of Germany's most prominent ecclesiastical structures and a UNESCO World Heritage Site. With its soaring towers, beautiful sculptures, and richly adorned interior, the Bamberg Cathedral exemplifies the city's religious legacy and architectural prowess.

In addition to cathedrals and town halls, Bamberg's Old Town contains a variety of historic churches, including the Michaelsberg Abbey, St. Martin's Church, and St. Jakob's Church. These medieval cathedrals boast breathtaking architecture, beautiful artwork, and centuries of religious history, making them must-see destinations for both history aficionados and architecture enthusiasts.

Bamberg's Old Town is especially known for its medieval bridges that connect the city's two rivers, the Regnitz and the Main. The Alte Mainbrücke, or Old Main Bridge, is one of Bamberg's oldest and most scenic bridges, with breathtaking views of the city skyline and surrounding countryside. Built in the 15th century, this historic bridge is embellished with statues of saints and religious figures, providing visitors with a magnificent visual spectacle.

In addition to its architectural landmarks, Bamberg's Old Town has a variety of historic palaces, residences, and public buildings, such as the Neue Residenz, Altenburg Castle, and Old Court. These large monuments provide glimpses into the city's noble heritage and aristocratic past, with luxurious interiors, attractive gardens, and fascinating displays that highlight Bamberg's rich cultural history.

Whether you're exploring the city's ancient cathedrals, strolling through its meandering alleyways, or admiring its old bridges and palaces, Bamberg's Old Town is a treasure trove of historical sites waiting to be explored.

Architectural Highlights

Bamberg's Old Town is well-known for its spectacular architecture, which spans centuries and includes a wide range of architectural styles, including Romanesque, Gothic, Baroque and Rococo. Bamberg's architectural attractions, which range from grand cathedrals and ancient churches to attractive squares and half-timbered houses, reflect the city's rich cultural and artistic tradition.

Bamberg Cathedral: One of the architectural highlights of Bamberg's Old Town is the Bamberg Cathedral, a Romanesque masterpiece and one of Germany's most prominent ecclesiastical monuments. The cathedral, constructed in the 11th century, has a spectacular facade covered with complex sculptures and carvings, as well as a highly decorated interior with beautiful murals, paintings, and stained glass windows. The Bamberg Cathedral, with its soaring spires and grand domes, is awe-inspiring and a must-see for architecture fans.

Altes Rathaus: Another architectural jewel in Bamberg's Old Town is the Altes Rathaus, or Old Town Hall, a remarkable structure located on a bridge above the Regnitz River. The Altes Rathaus, constructed in the 14th century, is a masterpiece of medieval architecture and a symbol of the city's civic pride. Its magnificent front, covered with vivid frescoes and elaborate carvings, is one of Bamberg's most famous sights and a popular tourist destination.

In addition to its cathedrals and town halls, Bamberg's Old Town houses a variety of historic churches, each with its own distinct architectural elements and artistic embellishments. These medieval buildings, ranging from the Michaelsberg Abbey with its Romanesque cloisters and Baroque interiors to St. Martin's Church with its Gothic spires and elaborate stone carvings, provide insight into Bamberg's religious legacy and architectural prowess.

Bamberg's Old Town is also known for its picturesque half-timbered buildings that line the city's small streets and alleys. These historic buildings, which date back to the Middle Ages, have colorful facades, wooden beams, and ornate motifs, providing a magnificent setting for visiting Bamberg's Old Town. Walking along the cobblestone streets, tourists may see the traditional houses' unique architecture and craftsmanship, which have been meticulously preserved for decades.

One of the architectural highlights of Bamberg's Old Town is the Klein-Venedig, or Little Venice, sector, which is a lovely enclave of half-timbered homes along the Regnitz River. Klein-Venedig, named after the famous Italian city, is a popular tourist destination, with charming canals, picturesque bridges, and waterfront cafes providing a peaceful retreat from the rush and bustle of the city center.

In addition to ancient buildings and churches, Bamberg's Old Town contains several architectural landmarks from the Baroque and Rococo periods. The Neue Residenz, or New Residence, is a notable example of Baroque architecture, with beautiful facades, huge staircases, and opulent interiors that reflect the wealth and power of Bamberg's rulers. The Residenz also features the spectacular Rose Garden, a terraced garden with panoramic views of the city, which is a favorite destination for visitors looking to appreciate Bamberg's architectural legacy.

Whether you're admiring the stately churches, wandering the meandering alleyways and lanes, or admiring the colorful half-timbered buildings, Bamberg's Old Town has a wealth of architectural marvels waiting to be explored. Bamberg's Old Town, with its rich history, numerous architectural styles, and spectacular landmarks, is a fascinating peek into the city's past as well as a visual feast for architecture fans.

Walking Tours

Walking tours are one of the best ways to visit Bamberg's Old Town, since they provide a complete overview of the city's history, architecture, and cultural heritage. Whether you're into medieval history, Gothic architecture, or local mythology and folklore, there's a walking tour for everyone. Below are some of the most popular walking tours in Bamberg's Old Town:

Historic City Center Trip: This trip, conducted by knowledgeable guides, takes visitors through Bamberg's historic city center, highlighting the city's most prominent sites such as the Bamberg Cathedral, Altes Rathaus, and Klein-Venedig area. Along the route, you'll discover the city's rich history, cultural legacy, and architectural significance, as well as insights into Bamberg's medieval past and contemporary life.

Beer And Brewery Tour: Bamberg is well-known for its beer culture, with nine breweries producing a wide range of traditional brews, including the world-renowned Rauchbier (smoked beer). This trip takes guests behind the scenes of Bamberg's breweries, where they can learn about the brewing process, try different beers, and explore the city's brewing traditions and customs. This trip, which includes visits to historic brewhouses as well as modern craft brewers, provides an overview of Bamberg's beer culture and gastronomic offerings.

Night Watchman Tour: Take a step back in time on this atmospheric tour conducted by a costumed night watchman who tells tourists about Bamberg's medieval history, folklore, and mysteries. As you travel around the Old Town's shadowy streets and alleys, you'll hear stories of witch hunts, eerie apparitions, and ancient rituals, giving you a unique perspective on Bamberg's history and traditions.

Architectural Heritage Tour: This tour takes architecture fans on a fascinating journey through Bamberg's architectural past, examining its various styles and influences, ranging from Romanesque and Gothic to Baroque and Rococo. This trip, led by expert experts, visits the city's most recognizable sites, such as cathedrals, churches, palaces, and half-timbered houses, and provides insights into the history of Bamberg's built environment throughout the years.

Art And Culture Tour: This tour brings visitors to museums, galleries, and cultural organizations that showcase Bamberg's artistic heritage and creative energy. From modern art exhibitions to traditional folk music performances, this tour provides an overview of Bamberg's cultural landscape and contributions to the arts.

Whether you're into history, architecture, beer, or art, there's a walking tour in Bamberg's Old Town to suit your interests. With experienced guides, engaging experiences, and captivating stories, these excursions provide a one-of-a-kind approach to discover the city's rich legacy and lively culture, leaving you with memories to cherish for years to come.

In this chapter, we looked at the delights of Bamberg's Old Town, including its UNESCO World Heritage Site status, historical sites, architectural highlights, and fascinating walking tours. Bamberg's Old Town, with its grand cathedrals and medieval churches, attractive half-timbered buildings, and busy market squares, provides a fascinating peek into the city's rich history, cultural heritage, and architectural legacy. Whether you're meandering through its winding alleyways, admiring its gorgeous architecture, or immersing yourself in its bustling environment, Bamberg's Old Town will make an indelible impression and stimulate your sense of wonder.

CHAPTER 5

BAMBERG' CULTURAL SCENE

Bamberg's vibrant cultural environment reflects the city's rich history, artistic heritage, and energetic community. From museums and galleries that highlight the city's rich history and artistic achievements to performing arts facilities that stage world-class performances, Bamberg has a plethora of cultural activities for visitors to enjoy. In this chapter, we'll look at Bamberg's rich cultural offerings, including museums, galleries, performing arts venues, and cultural events.

Museums And Galleries

Bamberg is home to numerous museums and galleries that provide unique insights into the city's history, art, and culture. Whether you're interested in medieval antiquities, modern art, or local folklore, Bamberg has a museum or gallery to fit your interests. Here are some must-see museums and galleries in Bamberg:

Bamberg State Library: Located in the former Jesuit College, the Bamberg State Library houses an extensive collection of rare books, manuscripts, and historical documents going back to the Middle Ages. Visitors can tour the library's stunning Baroque halls and galleries, which house treasures including illuminated manuscripts, early printed books, and historic maps.

Historical Museum Bamberg: Located in the Alte Hofhaltung, the Historical Museum Bamberg provides a thorough account of the city's history, from medieval times to the present. The museum's exhibitions include a wide range of topics, including archaeology, art, architecture, and everyday life, giving visitors a sense of Bamberg's rich cultural legacy and diversity.

Villa Concordia: This modern art gallery displays works by both local and international artists, with changing exhibitions of painting, sculpture, photography, and multimedia installations. Villa Concordia, located in a historic villa overlooking the Regnitz River, provides a peaceful setting for discovering modern art and connecting with the local creative community.

Diocesan Museum Bamberg: Adjacent to the Bamberg Cathedral, the Diocesan Museum Bamberg exhibits a collection of religious items, artworks, and treasures from the Catholic Church. Highlights include medieval sculptures, altarpieces, and religious relics, as well as displays about the history of the Bamberg Diocese and its influence on the city's cultural character.

Franconian Brewery Museum: Beer enthusiasts will want to pay a visit to the Franconian Brewery Museum, which highlights the history and legacy of brewing in Bamberg and the surrounding area. The museum's exhibits cover brewing techniques, beer production, and the cultural relevance of beer in Franconian society, as well as tastings and guided tours of local breweries.

These are just a few of the many museums and galleries waiting to be discovered in Bamberg. Whether you're into art, history, or beer, you'll find something to tickle your interest and broaden your awareness of Bamberg's cultural scene.

Performing Arts Venues

Bamberg has a vibrant performing arts scene, with theaters, music halls, and opera houses hosting a variety of productions throughout the year. From classical music concerts and opera performances to contemporary theater and dance productions, Bamberg's performing arts venues provide something for everyone. Here are some of the best venues to check out:

E.T.A. Hoffmann Theater: Named after the great German writer and composer E.T.A. Hoffmann, this theater features a variety of productions such as plays, musicals, and ballets. The E.T.A. Hoffmann Theater, with its historic location and diversified programming, serves as a cultural hub for theater fans in Bamberg.

Konzerthalle Bamberg: This sophisticated performance venue is home to the Bamberg Symphony Orchestra, one of Germany's top orchestras. The Konzerthalle Bamberg provides regular concerts that include classical music, modern works, and guest appearances by renowned soloists and conductors. With its cutting-edge acoustics and exquisite design, it's a must-see for music fans in Bamberg.

Kunstlerhaus Im Erba-Park: This cultural center presents a wide variety of performing arts, including theater, dance, music, and multimedia acts. With its intimate theater rooms, experimental programming, and emphasis on contemporary art forms, the Kunstlerhaus im Erba-Park provides a platform for new artists and unique shows in Bamberg.

Bamberg Puppet Theater: Established in 1946, the Bamberg Puppet Theater is one of Germany's oldest puppet theaters, entertaining audiences of all ages with its enchanting puppetry presentations. From classic fairy tales and children's stories to unique shows and puppet workshops, the theater provides a fascinating experience for people of all ages.

These are just a handful of Bamberg's many performing arts facilities, each of which provides distinct experiences and opportunities to connect with the local arts community. Whether you prefer classical music, contemporary theatre, or experimental performance art, Bamberg's thriving cultural scene has something for everyone.

Cultural Activities And Festivals

Throughout the year, Bamberg hosts a number of cultural events and festivals that honor the city's rich history, artistic inventiveness, and community spirit. From traditional folk festivals and music performances to modern art exhibitions and gourmet fairs, there is always something going on in Bamberg to keep tourists entertained and inspired. Here are some of the biggest cultural events and festivals to watch out for.

Sandkerwa: Held every August, Sandkerwa is Bamberg's largest and most popular folk festival, drawing thousands of people from near and far. The festival includes live music, traditional dancing, food and drink vendors, carnival rides, and a lively atmosphere that energizes the Old Town streets.

Bamberg Jazz Festival: Jazz fans will not want to miss the Bamberg Jazz Festival, which combines top international jazz performers with local talent for a week of performances, jam sessions, workshops, and special activities. From smooth jazz to avant-garde improvisation, the festival has something for jazz fans of all interests and inclinations.

Bamberg Kulturbiergarten: This open-air cultural beer garden provides a relaxed setting in which visitors may enjoy live music, theater performances, film screenings, and art exhibitions while drinking local beer and enjoying regional cuisine. With its picturesque setting along the riverfront, the Kulturbiergarten is a favorite gathering place for both locals and tourists.

Bamberg International Film Festival: Film enthusiasts will enjoy the Bamberg International Film Festival, which features a broad range of independent films, documentaries, and short films from all over the world. The festival includes screenings, Q&A sessions with filmmakers, panel discussions, and special events, allowing cinephiles to discover new talent and connect with the global film community.

Bamberg Christmas Market: During the holiday season, Bamberg's Old Town changes into a winter paradise with the annual Christmas Market, also known as Weihnachtsmarkt. Visitors can explore festive stalls selling homemade crafts, traditional presents, and seasonal refreshments while listening to live music, singing carols, and watching local artists perform. The Bamberg Christmas Market, with its dazzling lights, scented mulled wine, and seasonal decorations, provides a delightful experience for visitors of all ages.

These are just a few of the many cultural events and festivals held in Bamberg throughout the year, each of which provides unique opportunity to immerse yourself in the city's dynamic cultural scene and connect with its rich legacy and traditions. Bamberg's numerous cultural events and festivals offer something for everyone, whether you prefer music, theater, film, or gastronomic delights.

In this chapter, we looked at Bamberg's vibrant cultural landscape, which includes museums, galleries, performing arts venues, and exciting festivals. Whether you're admiring medieval treasures in a museum, listening to classical music in a famous concert hall, or celebrating with locals at a festive event, Bamberg has a rich tapestry of cultural experiences waiting to be found. Bamberg is a location where creativity thrives and traditions are treasured, allowing visitors to explore, engage, and be inspired by its distinctive cultural offers.

CHAPTER 6

DINING IN BAMBERG

Bamberg's culinary culture reflects its rich cultural past and Bavarian traditions. From substantial Bavarian delicacies served in quaint taverns to creative food created by outstanding chefs, the city has a wide range of eating alternatives to suit any taste. In this chapter, we'll look at Bamberg's dining options, including traditional Bavarian cuisine as well as local restaurants, cafes, and specialty food stores.

Traditional Bavarian Cuisine

Bavarian cuisine is known for its rich, comforting dishes, which frequently use locally produced ingredients and time-honored recipes passed down through generations. Visitors to Bamberg can experience Bavarian cuisine at classic taverns, beer gardens, and restaurants located around the city. Here are some traditional Bavarian foods to sample during your stay to Bamberg.

Schäufele: A Bavarian specialty, this roasted pork shoulder has tender, juicy flesh with crispy skin and is served with dumplings, sauerkraut, and gravy. It's a rich and filling dinner ideal for sharing with friends and family.

Bratwurst: No trip to Bamberg is complete without sampling the city's famed bratwurst, which is created with finely ground pork seasoned with a blend of spices and herbs and grilled to perfection. To complete the Bavarian experience, serve with sauerkraut, mustard, and a freshly made pretzel.

Haxen: This traditional dish consists of roasted pork knuckle marinated and slow-cooked till soft, served with potato dumplings, red cabbage, and sauce. It's a meaty and savory dish that'll satisfy even the most voracious appetite.

Kartoffelsalat: Bavarian potato salad is a simple but tasty side dish made with boiled potatoes, onions, and a tangy vinaigrette dressing. It makes an excellent addition to any Bavarian meal, particularly grilled meats, sausages, and schnitzel.

Käsespätzle: This Bavarian version of macaroni and cheese has soft egg noodles covered with melted cheese, caramelized onions, and crunchy breadcrumbs. It's a delicious and cozy dish that will keep you warm on a cold day.

Apfelstrudel: For dessert, try a slice of Bavarian apple strudel, which is a flaky pastry filled with cinnamon-spiced apples and raisins and served warm with whipped cream or vanilla ice cream. It adds a delicious and delightful finish to any meal.

These are just a few of the numerous excellent foods available in Bamberg. Whether you're looking for substantial comfort food or inventive cuisine, you'll find something to satisfy your palate in this gastronomic paradise.

Local Restaurants And Cafés

In addition to traditional taverns and beer gardens, Bamberg has a thriving dining scene with a vast selection of restaurants, cafes, and eateries serving a variety of cuisines and culinary experiences. From small bistros serving homemade specialties to elegant eateries exhibiting creative food, Bamberg has something for everyone's taste and preferences. Here are some excellent recommendations for eating out in the city.

Spezial-Keller: Located on the slopes of Michaelsberg Hill, Spezial-Keller is a historic beer garden with panoramic views of the city and a laid-back environment. Visitors can savor traditional Bavarian meals, grilled meats, and locally brewed beers while taking in the breathtaking environment and welcoming atmosphere.

Schlenkerla: This landmark brewery and restaurant is famous for its smoked beer, or Rauchbier, which is made with traditional methods and smoked over beechwood fires. Visitors can experience Schlenkerla's smoked beers, as well as substantial Bavarian meals like schäufele, bratwurst, and sauerkraut, in the warm beer hall or outdoor beer garden.

Wirtshaus Schäferhalle: A quaint tavern in Bamberg's Old Town that serves authentic Bavarian food with a modern touch. Dishes are made with locally sourced ingredients and traditional traditions, with a focus on quality and flavor. Visitors can dine in the intimate dining room or outside on the terrace, with views of the old buildings and bustling streets.

Café Müller: For a taste of Bamberg's café culture, visit Café Müller, a quiet coffeehouse that serves freshly brewed coffee, handcrafted pastries, and light fare. Visitors can unwind in the beautiful interior or outside courtyard while sipping cappuccinos and sampling exquisite desserts and tarts made with local ingredients.

Kachelofen: This family-run restaurant serves Franconian food, including regional delicacies like schnitzel, krenfleisch, and karpfen. The dishes are made with care and attention to detail, using traditional recipes and seasonal ingredients gathered from local farmers and producers.

These are just a few of the many restaurants and cafes available in Bamberg. Whether you're looking for traditional Bavarian fare, cosmopolitan cuisine, or gourmet pleasures, you'll find something to suit your taste in this culinary hub.

Specialty Food Market

Bamberg is a foodie's and culinary enthusiast's dream, with specialist food markets, delis, and gourmet shops selling a delectable selection of local and artisanal items. These markets are a feast for the senses, offering everything from fresh fruit and meats to cheese, bread, and sweets. They are a must-see for anybody looking to sample the finest Bavarian food. Here are some of the best specialty food markets in Bamberg:

Bamberg Farmers' Market: Held weekly in the city center, the Bamberg Farmers' Market is a thriving hub of activity where visitors may explore stalls selling fresh fruits and vegetables, meats, cheeses, and baked items from local farmers and producers. With its bright environment and varied product variety, it's ideal for stocking up on picnic goods or gathering things for a gourmet supper at home.

Frische Paradies Bamberg: This gourmet market offers a diverse selection of high-quality products, including fresh seafood, meats, cheeses, and specialized ingredients supplied from all over the world. Visitors can peruse the aisles, sample gourmet goodies, and speak with educated employees who can make recommendations and provide cooking tips.

Bamberger Wochenmarkt: Located on the historic Maximiliansplatz, the Bamberger Wochenmarkt is a weekly market with a variety of merchants selling fresh fruit, flowers, meats, cheeses, and handmade goods. Visitors can walk through the market, taking in the views, smells, and sounds of the bustling stalls while purchasing locally grown fruits and vegetables, homemade jams and preserves, and other culinary pleasures.

Metzgerei Dürr: This family-owned butcher shop has been serving Bamberg inhabitants for decades, offering a diverse assortment of fresh meats, sausages, and prepared dishes created from traditional recipes and high-quality ingredients. The Metzgerei Dürr shop sells Bavarian favorites including bratwurst, schäufele, and Leberkäse, as well as house-made salads, sandwiches, and ready-to-eat meals.

Käse-Laden Bamberg: Cheese aficionados will want to pay a visit to Käse-Laden Bamberg, a specialized cheese shop that offers a diverse assortment of artisanal cheeses from Bavaria and elsewhere. Visitors can try a variety of cheeses, from creamy bries and zesty blues to aged goudas and smokey alpines, and speak with trained staff who can make recommendations and pairing suggestions.

Bäckerei Konditorei Müller: For over a century, this traditional bakery and pastry business has delighted Bamberg locals with its freshly baked breads, pastries, and cakes. Visitors can indulge in a morning croissant, midday cake, or freshly made loaf of bread and taste the flavors of Bavarian baking at its peak.

Feinkostladen Wagner: This gourmet delicatessen sells a variety of specialty foods, including cured meats, cheeses, olives, oils, and vinegars, as well as gourmet pantry basics like pasta, sauces, and condiments. Visitors can stock up on gourmet supplies for home cooking or choose from a variety of pre-made dishes and snacks for a picnic or dinner party.

These specialist food markets and stores are a treasure trove of culinary delights, allowing tourists to sample the best of Bavarian cuisine and artisan products. Whether you're looking for fresh ingredients, gourmet snacks, or one-of-a-kind mementos to take home, Bamberg's dynamic food scene is guaranteed to satisfy your palate.

In this chapter, we looked at Bamberg's broad culinary scene, from traditional Bavarian cuisine to local restaurants, cafes, and specialty food stores. Whether you're indulging in hearty schäufele and bratwurst at a traditional tavern, sipping coffee and nibbling on pastries at a cozy cafe, or browsing stalls of fresh produce and artisanal products at a farmers' market, Bamberg provides a gastronomic adventure that will delight food lovers of all tastes and preferences. Bamberg, with its rich culinary tradition, dynamic food scene, and friendly hospitality, welcomes guests to eat, drink, and relish Bavarian delicacies in every bite.

CHAPTER 7

NIGHTLIFE IN BAMBERG

Bamberg's nightlife scene is as diverse as the city itself, with options for everyone, whether they prefer quaint pubs, boisterous bars, or vibrant live music places. From traditional beer halls selling local brews to elegant wine bars pouring rare vintages, Bamberg comes alive after dark with a plethora of alternatives for entertainment and networking. In this chapter, we will look at Bamberg's nightlife attractions, which include bars, pubs, wine bars, beer gardens, and live music venues.

Bars And Pub

Bamberg has a bustling bar and pub culture, with locations ranging from medieval taverns to fashionable cocktail bars, each with its own distinct atmosphere and menu of drinks. Whether you want a typical Bavarian beer or an innovative specialty drink, there are lots of alternatives in Bamberg's taverns and pubs. Here are some excellent recommendations for a night out on the town:

Schlenkerla: This historic brewery and tavern is famous for its smoked beer, or Rauchbier, which is made with traditional methods and smoked over beechwood fires. Visitors can enjoy a pint of Schlenkerla's famous beer in the snug beer hall or the outdoor beer garden while taking in the lively ambiance and enjoying substantial Bavarian delicacies like schäufele and bratwurst.

Griefenklau Brauerei: Located in a lovely nook of Bamberg's Old Town, Griefenklau Brauerei is a family-owned brewery and bar famed for its traditional Franconian brews and friendly service. Visitors can unwind in the rustic beer garden or comfortable interior, sipping freshly brewed beers and snacking on homemade treats while mingling with locals and other tourists.

Altstadtbar: Located in the heart of Bamberg's historic city, Altstadtbar is a popular gathering place for both locals and visitors, with a relaxed environment and a diverse selection of drinks. Whether you want a cool beer, a glass of wine, or a traditional cocktail, you can find it here, along with pleasant service and a welcome atmosphere.

Fässla: This family-run brewery and bar has been serving Bamberg inhabitants for decades, with a warm environment and a selection of traditional Franconian beers. Visitors can experience Fässla's brews, including its famed Kellerbier, in the rustic beer hall or outdoor beer garden, which are served alongside substantial Bavarian meals and fresh pretzels.

Café Abseits: This stylish bar and cafe is a popular hangout for Bamberg's younger set, with a laid-back ambiance, innovative cocktails, and a rotating range of craft beer. Café Abseits, with its quirky decor, friendly staff, and lively atmosphere, is the ideal place to unwind with friends after a hard day of touring the city.

Whether you prefer a traditional beer hall experience or a modern cocktail bar, Bamberg's bars and pubs cater to every taste and inclination, inviting tourists to raise a glass and toast to a fantastic night out in this picturesque Bavarian city.

Wine Bars And Beer Garden

In addition to traditional beer halls and pubs, Bamberg has a number of wine bars and beer gardens where tourists may taste local wines, beers, and spirits in beautiful outdoor settings. From vine-covered courtyards to riverbank terraces, these places provide the ideal setting for sipping a drink al fresco while taking in the splendor of Bamberg. Here are some of the city's top wine bars and beer gardens:

Stöhrenkeller: Nestled in the hills above Bamberg, this medieval beer garden provides panoramic views of the city and surrounding countryside. Visitors can relax in the covered beer garden, sipping locally made beers and eating typical Franconian delicacies like bratwurst and pretzels while admiring the breathtaking views.

Weinstube Baldreit: A picturesque half-timbered structure in Bamberg's Old Town has a quaint wine bar that specializes in Franconian wines and regional dishes. Visitors can enjoy a large selection of local vintages combined with cheese, charcuterie, and other gourmet delicacies, all while taking in the comfortable environment and rustic beauty of the historic location.

Bamberger Weinhaus: This wine bar and shop serves a carefully curated variety of wines from Bamberg and the surrounding Franconia area, as well as expert advice and recommendations from knowledgeable personnel. Visitors can try wines by the glass or bottle, surrounded by a selection of cheese and antipasti, before perusing the shop's shelves for bottles to take home as keepsakes.

Gasthausbrauerei Brauerei Greifenklau: In addition to its brewery and beer garden, Brauerei Greifenklau has a charming wine bar where guests can try a selection of local wines, spirits, and liqueurs. With its welcoming ambiance, pleasant service, and large drink selection, it's the ideal place to relax with a glass of wine after a day of sightseeing in Bamberg.

These wine bars and beer gardens provide a relaxing and pleasant atmosphere for experiencing the flavors of Franconia and taking in the splendor of Bamberg, making them ideal for an evening of leisurely beverages and chat with friends.

Live Music Venues

Bamberg has a variety of live music venues where tourists may see performances by local bands, visiting artists, and talented musicians from all over the world. From tiny jazz clubs to vibrant concert halls, these venues present a wide range of musical genres and styles, guaranteeing that there is always something exciting going on in the city's music scene. Here are some of the top live music venues in Bamberg:

Live-Club Bamberg: Located in the heart of Bamberg's Old Town, Live-Club Bamberg is a prominent live music venue with a calendar full of concerts, gigs, and events spanning a wide spectrum of musical genres, including rock and pop, jazz, blues, and electronic music. It's a popular hangout for music fans of all interests and inclinations, thanks to its intimate setting, cutting-edge sound system, and diversified programming.

Jazzclub Bamberg: This intimate jazz club features regular concerts by local jazz bands, touring acts, and worldwide performers, highlighting the best of the local jazz scene while also offering a platform for up-and-coming musicians to display their talents. Jazzclub Bamberg, with its relaxed atmosphere and compact location, provides a one-of-a-kind and memorable live music experience for both jazz enthusiasts and casual listeners.

Sound-N-Arts Music Club: This hip music club hosts a broad mix of live bands and DJs who perform everything from indie rock and alternative to hip hop and electronic dance music. Sound-n-Arts Music Club is a popular hangout for Bamberg's young and stylish audience, delivering a dynamic and energetic nightlife experience that will keep you moving.

Kellerperle: Located in a historic cellar beneath Bamberg's streets, Kellerperle is a one-of-a-kind music venue that hosts regular concerts and events with local bands and artists. Kellerperle, with its underground setting, intimate atmosphere, and broad lineup of musical artists, provides a one-of-a-kind live music experience unlike any other in Bamberg. Visitors can drink at the bar while seeing performances by emerging musicians, veteran bands, and everything in between.

Brose Arena: Bamberg's primary facility for larger-scale concerts and events, presenting top international performers, touring bands, and big events year-round. Brose Arena, with its cutting-edge amenities, extensive seating, and excellent acoustics, provides a world-class musical experience that music fans visiting Bamberg should not miss.

Kulturkeller: This cultural center and music venue organizes a wide range of events, including concerts, theater performances, art exhibitions, and film screenings, highlighting the finest of Bamberg's arts and entertainment scene. Kulturkeller is a dynamic hub of cultural activity and a must-see location for anybody interested in experiencing Bamberg's creative energy.

These live music venues provide a wide range of musical experiences, from small jazz performances to high-energy rock concerts, guaranteeing that there is something for everyone to enjoy in Bamberg's bustling nightlife scene.

In this chapter, we looked at Bamberg's wide and active nightlife scene, which ranged from quaint pubs and wine bars to live music venues. Bamberg provides many chances for amusement and mingling after dark, whether you're sipping on a locally brewed beer in a historic beer hall, savoring a glass of wine in a quaint wine bar, or dancing the night away to live music in a trendy music club. Bamberg welcomes tourists to enjoy the city's bustling midnight scene and make experiences that will last a lifetime.

CHAPTER 8

OUTDOOR ACTIVITIES IN BAMBERG

Bamberg, with its gorgeous scenery, meandering rivers, and lush foliage, provides a multitude of outdoor activities for both nature lovers and outdoor enthusiasts. There are numerous options to explore the great outdoors in Bamberg, including calm parks and gardens, gorgeous cycling and hiking routes, and leisurely river cruises along the meandering canals. In this chapter, we'll look at the different outdoor activities that await tourists to this picturesque Bavarian city.

Parks And Gardens

Bamberg has various magnificent parks and gardens where tourists may get away from the hustle and bustle of the city and immerse themselves in nature's peace. Whether you're searching for a calm site for a leisurely stroll, a gorgeous picnic spot, or a place to relax and unwind, Bamberg's parks and gardens provide the ideal backdrop for outdoor activities. Here are some of the best parks and gardens to explore in Bamberg.

Hain Park: Hain Park, located on the banks of the River Regnitz, is Bamberg's largest and most popular park, with acres of lush greenery, meandering trails, and picturesque views of the river and surrounding countryside. Visitors can walk through woodland forests, relax on grassy lawns, or observe the park's magnificent gardens, fountains, and statues while taking in the views and sounds of nature.

Rosengarten: Located on the grounds of the New Residence palace, Rosengarten is a stunning rose garden with hundreds of rose varieties in bloom from spring to autumn. Visitors can walk through the fragrant rose gardens, observe the vibrant blossoms, and enjoy panoramic views of the city skyline and the magnificent Michaelsberg hill.

Bamberg Botanical Garden: Tucked away behind the university campus, the Bamberg Botanical Garden is a hidden gem worth visiting for its rich variety of plants, flowers, and trees from all over the world. Visitors can visit themed gardens like the alpine garden, medicinal herb garden, and tropical greenhouse to learn about plant diversity and conservation.

Margareteninsel: This picturesque island park is located in the middle of the River Regnitz and may be accessed via footbridges on both sides. Margareteninsel provides a tranquil escape from the city center, with leafy forests, grassy meadows, and riverbank promenades ideal for picnicking, sunbathing, or simply admiring the river vistas.

These parks and gardens provide a calm and attractive setting for outdoor activities such as strolling, jogging, cycling, or simply admiring nature's beauty, making them popular with both locals and visitors.

Cycling And Hiking Trails

Bamberg's picturesque scenery and network of rivers and canals make it a perfect location for cycling and trekking lovers seeking to experience the great outdoors. Bamberg's level terrain, well-maintained routes, and stunning landscape provide limitless options for outdoor adventure and exploration, whether on two wheels or on foot. Here are some of the best cycling and hiking trails to explore in and around Bamberg:

Regnitz Radweg: A popular cycling path that runs from Bamberg to Nuremberg along the River Regnitz, passing through gorgeous scenery, lovely villages, and ancient towns. The track, which stretches for more than 100 kilometers, is suited for cyclists of all skill levels and provides numerous opportunities to stop and visit areas of interest along the way.

Main-Donau Radweg: This long-distance cycling trail connects Germany's Main River with Austria's Danube River, passing through Bamberg along the way. The Main-Donau Radweg, which stretches for over 500 kilometers, provides stunning scenery, historic landmarks, and cultural attractions, making it a popular choice for multi-day cycling tours and leisurely day outings.

Franconian Switzerland: The Franconian Switzerland region, located just a short drive from Bamberg, is known for its rocky limestone cliffs, dense forests, and picturesque valleys. Outdoor enthusiasts will find a network of well-marked hiking trails leading to magnificent vistas, hidden caverns, and attractive villages, providing limitless opportunity for exploration and adventure in nature.

Bamberg Cycle Path: For a lovely bike ride closer to the city center, the Bamberg Cycle Path follows the banks of the River Regnitz, passing through parks, gardens, and historic buildings including the Old Town Hall, Little Venice, and Altenburg Castle. The flat and well-paved trail is ideal for cyclists of all ages and skill levels, providing a relaxed opportunity to view the sites and appreciate the beauty of Bamberg's riverfront setting.

Whether you're cycling along gorgeous riverbanks, hiking through lush forests, or discovering lovely villages and historic landmarks, Bamberg provides limitless chances for outdoor adventure and exploration, making it an ideal location for nature lovers and outdoor enthusiasts.

River Cruises

One of the greatest ways to see Bamberg's beautiful beauty and historic charm is to take a leisurely river cruise around the city's rivers. A river cruise, whether on the meandering River Regnitz, the calm Main-Danube Canal, or the vast Main River, provides a unique perspective of Bamberg's scenic landscapes, historic landmarks, and lovely riverside villages. Here are some of the best river cruises to take in Bamberg:

Regnitz River Trip: Board a traditional riverboat and embark on a scenic trip along the River Regnitz, passing past historic landmarks such as the Old Town Hall, Altenburg Castle, and the lovely fishermen's homes of Little Venice. A Regnitz River cruise is a must-do excursion for tourists to Bamberg, offering educational commentary from professional guides, breathtaking views of the city skyline, and several photo opportunities along the way.

Main-Danube Canal Cruise: Take a leisurely cruise through scenic countryside, past lush vineyards and lovely villages, and via historic locks and aqueducts. Learn about the canal's amazing history and engineering marvels as you glide over the water, soaking in the sights and sounds of Bavaria.

Main River Cruise: Take a picturesque river cruise along the Main River, one of Germany's longest and most scenic rivers, which runs through Bamberg on its way from the Franconian wine area to the Rhine. Enjoy magnificent views of the river valley, undulating hills, and vineyard-covered slopes, as well as historic castles, churches, and villages scattered throughout the countryside.

Bamberg Gondola Trip: For a really unforgettable and romantic experience, arrange a private gondola trip down the

River Regnitz, where you may glide through the river in a traditional Venetian-style gondola, complete with a gondolier dressed in traditional garb. Enjoy a bottle of wine or champagne as you pass by historic sites, scenic bridges, and charming waterfront cafés and restaurants.

These river excursions provide a pleasant and scenic opportunity to see the sites of Bamberg from a new perspective, making it a memorable experience for people of all ages and interests.

Whether you like wandering through lush parks and gardens, exploring gorgeous cycling and hiking routes, or taking a leisurely ride along the city's canals, Bamberg has limitless chances for outdoor adventure and discovery. With its spectacular natural beauty, ancient sites, and lovely riverfront landscape, Bamberg is the ideal place for nature lovers and outdoor enthusiasts wishing to immerse themselves in the great outdoors.

In this chapter, we've looked at the various outdoor activities offered in Bamberg, including calm parks and gardens, gorgeous cycling and hiking routes, and relaxing river cruises along the city's waterways. Whether you're looking for relaxation, adventure, or just a chance to reconnect with nature, Bamberg has something for everyone in its magnificent outdoor landscapes and historic surrounds. So put on your hiking boots, take your bike, or board a boat and prepare to enjoy the beauty and charm of Bamberg's wonderful outdoors.

CHAPTER 9

DAY TRIPS FROM BAMBERG

Bamberg's central location in the heart of Franconia gives it an excellent starting point for exploring the surrounding area, which is filled with attractive towns and villages, rolling vineyards, and medieval castles. From beautiful drives through the lovely countryside to guided tours of medieval fortifications and wine tastings in charming wineries, there are numerous options for fascinating day trips from Bamberg. In this chapter, we will look at some of the best day trip sites for travelers who want to discover Franconia's beauty and legacy.

Nearby Towns And Villages

Franconia is full with attractive towns and villages, each with its own history, culture, and attractions waiting to be discovered. From historic walled cities to lovely riverbank villages, there are many of places to visit just a short drive or rail ride from Bamberg. Here are a few recommendations for local towns and villages to visit:

Forchheim: Forchheim, known as the "Gateway to Franconian Switzerland," is a historic town with a well-preserved medieval core that includes half-timbered homes, cobblestone streets, and a lovely town hall square. Visitors can wander along the picturesque riverfront promenade and discover the town's small shops, cafes, and museums.

Bayreuth: Known for its yearly Wagner Festival and rich cultural heritage, Bayreuth is a lively city with a flourishing arts scene, historic sites, and lovely parks and gardens. Visitors can take a tour of the opulent Margravial Opera House, see the historic Old Town, and learn about the famed composer's life and works at the Richard Wagner Museum.

Coburg: Located in the foothills of the Thuringian Forest, Coburg is a lovely town with a fairy-tale castle, medieval old town, and charming market squares. Visitors can tour the impressive Veste Coburg fortification, see the town's museums and galleries, and wander through the picturesque Hofgarten park.

Würzburg: Only an hour's drive from Bamberg, Würzburg is a medieval city with spectacular baroque architecture, including the UNESCO-listed Residenz Palace and the Marienberg Fortress. Visitors can explore the picturesque Old Town, walk along the scenic Main River promenade, and try local wines at one of the city's numerous wine bars and taverns.

These surrounding towns and villages provide a look into Franconia's rich cultural past while also offering a lovely getaway from the hustle and bustle of city life, making them ideal day trip options for visitors to Bamberg.

Franconian Wine Country

Franconia is known for its wine-producing region, which includes some of Germany's finest vineyards and wineries. With its rolling hills, sunny slopes, and excellent soil, the location is perfect for growing a wide range of grape varietals, including Silvaner, Müller-Thurgau, and Riesling. Visitors to Bamberg can go on a wine-tasting journey through Franconian wine country, taste award-winning wines, touring historic vineyards, and taking in the stunning landscape along the way. Here are some good destinations for discovering Franconian wine country:

Volkach: Located on the banks of the Main River, Volkach is recognized as the "Gateway to the Main Valley Wine Region" and is home to various vineyards and estates. Visitors can explore the town's old wine cellars, drink local wines at the annual "Volkacher Weinfrühling" wine festival, and take picturesque boat trips down the Main River.

Iphofen: This picturesque wine village is known for its medieval city walls, historic churches, and quaint town center. Visitors can wander through the town's vineyards, visit local wineries for tastings and tours, and eat traditional Franconian cuisine at cozy wine taverns and gastropubs.

Würzburg Wine Region: Located just a short drive from Bamberg, the Würzburg wine region is one of Franconia's most prominent wine-growing regions, famed for its picturesque vineyards, historic wine estates, and award-winning wines. Visitors can explore the region's vineyards and wineries, sample local vintages at wine festivals and tastings, and learn about the winemaking process from expert vintners.

Wine Road Franconia: Spanning over 500 kilometers through the heart of Franconia, the Wine Road Franconia is a scenic route that weaves past vineyards, orchards, and picturesque villages, providing spectacular views as well as numerous possibilities for wine sampling and exploration. Visitors can travel the Wine Road by vehicle, bike, or foot, stopping at wineries, restaurants, and historical sites along the way.

A day trip to Franconian wine country provides a unique opportunity to appreciate the region's flavors, enjoy the hospitality of local winemakers, and immerse oneself in the beauty of the countryside, making it a must-do activity for both wine fans and foodies.

Castle Tours

Franconia is home to numerous medieval castles and fortifications, each with its own distinct history, architectural style, and cultural significance. There are plenty of castles to explore in the region, ranging from intimidating hilltop strongholds to lovely royal gardens. Visitors to Bamberg can take a castle tour, seeing some of Franconia's most renowned monuments and immersing themselves in the region's rich history. Here are some popular castle tours to consider:

Altenburg Castle: Perched on a hill overlooking Bamberg, Altenburg Castle is a medieval castle with a 1,000-year history. Visitors can explore the castle's medieval walls, towers, and dungeons, as well as the museum exhibits showing items and archeological finds from the castle's past. They can also enjoy panoramic views of the city and surrounding countryside from the battlements.

Burg Pottenstein: Located in the heart of Franconian Switzerland, Burg Pottenstein is a gorgeous hilltop castle with a fairy-tale setting that overlooks the charming village of Pottenstein. Visitors can tour the castle's well-preserved remains, visit the museum displays that trace the castle's history and legend, and take scenic walks into the surrounding forest and farmland.

Rosenburg Castle: Located in the lovely town of Rödental, Rosenburg Castle is a Renaissance-style palace surrounded by wonderfully landscaped gardens and parklands. Visitors can explore the castle's luxurious interiors, including the elaborately adorned apartments, the medieval armory, and the impressive collection of art and antiques, as well as wander around the castle gardens, which offer panoramic views of the surrounding countryside.

Veste Coburg: Located on a rocky hilltop above Coburg, Veste Coburg is one of Germany's largest and best-preserved medieval strongholds. Visitors can explore the castle's majestic walls, towers, and courtyards, as well as the museum exhibits highlighting the castle's history and treasures. They can also enjoy panoramic views of the town and surrounding terrain from the castle's battlements.

A castle tour provides an intriguing view into Franconia's medieval past, transporting tourists back in time to witness the grandeur and romance of the region's historic fortifications and palaces. From discovering historic battlements and secret corridors to admiring rare art collections and taking in panoramic views of the landscape, a castle tour promises an exciting journey through Franconia's rich history and legacy.

In this chapter, we've looked at some of the best day trip locations from Bamberg, including surrounding towns and villages, Franconian wine area, and historical castles. Whether you're wandering through medieval streets, sipping wine in a picturesque vineyard, or exploring the grand halls of a centuries-old fortress, each of these day trips provide a unique opportunity to learn about Franconia's beauty, culture, and history, making them ideal additions to any itinerary for Bamberg visitors. So pack your luggage, lace on your hiking boots, and prepare to start on an incredible journey through this picturesque region's charming towns, rolling vineyards, and historic sites.

CHAPTER 10

SHOPPING IN BAMBERG

Bamberg, with its rich history and dynamic culture, provides a great shopping experience for travelers who want to discover its unique stores, markets, and boutiques. There's something for everyone to discover in Bamberg's unique retail scene, which includes lovely souvenir shops stocked with traditional Bavarian trinkets, lively markets teeming with local produce and artisanal goods, and contemporary fashion boutiques displaying the latest trends. In this chapter, we will look at the best shopping venues in this charming Bavarian city.

Souvenir Shops

No trip to Bamberg is complete without purchasing a few mementos to remember your stay in this wonderful city. Bamberg's souvenir stores sell a variety of typical Bavarian souvenirs including as beer steins, cuckoo clocks, lederhosen, and dirndls, as well as locally manufactured handicrafts, ceramics, and woodcarvings. Whether you're looking for a unique souvenir from your vacation or a memorable gift for friends and family back home, Bamberg's souvenir stores have you covered. Here are some excellent choices for souvenir buying in Bamberg:

Bamberg Souvenir Shop: Located in the center of the Old Town, this popular souvenir shop sells a variety of typical Bavarian goods and memorabilia such as beer steins, fridge magnets, postcards, and more. Visitors can peruse shelves full of souvenirs showcasing renowned Bamberg landmarks such as the Old Town Hall, Altenburg Castle, and the Little Venice neighborhood, and take home a few mementos of their visit to this historic city.

Bamberger Landmarkt: This beautiful shop sells locally manufactured handicrafts and artisanal products like hand-painted ceramics, wooden toys, handmade jewelry, and fabrics. Visitors can explore shelves full of one-of-a-kind goods created by local artists and purchase a piece of Bamberg's cultural legacy to take home as a souvenir of their visit.

Bamberg Christmas Market: During the holiday season, the city is transformed into a festive wonderland, with stalls selling a variety of traditional Christmas decorations, ornaments, and gifts. Visitors can stroll through the market's glittering lights, inhale the aroma of mulled wine and roasted chestnuts, and browse for homemade crafts, toys, and sweets to celebrate the season in style.

These souvenir stores provide a beautiful selection of presents and keepsakes to suit every taste and budget, ensuring that guests can find the ideal memory of their stay to Bamberg to treasure for years to come.

Local Markets And Artisanal Products

For those looking to discover Bamberg's unique culinary delights and artisanal products, the city's markets are a treasure trove of fresh produce, gourmet snacks, and handmade goods. From bustling farmers' markets to tiny craft fairs, there are plenty of opportunities to experience the finest of Bamberg's local flavors and workmanship. Here are some excellent locations for market shopping in Bamberg:

Bamberg Farmers' Market: Held weekly in the city center, the farmers' market is a bustling event with vendors selling a variety of fresh fruits and vegetables, artisanal cheeses, meats, baked products, and more. Visitors can interact with local farmers and producers, sample seasonal specialties, and purchase supplies for a picnic or gourmet supper.

Fischmarkt: A scenic plaza surrounded by ancient buildings and busy market booths on the banks of the River Regnitz. Visitors can peruse stalls selling fresh fish and shellfish, local delicacies like smoked trout and marinated herring, and handmade jams, honey, and preserves.

Bamberg Artisan Market: The Bamberg Artisan Market is held on a regular basis throughout the year and highlights the work of local craftsmen and artists, such as pottery, ceramics, textiles, jewelry, and woodwork. Visitors can peruse stalls full of one-of-a-kind and handcrafted things, speak with craftsmen about their trade, and purchase one-of-a-kind souvenirs and gifts to take home.

These markets provide a colorful and unique shopping experience, allowing visitors to interact with local producers and artists while sampling the best of Bamberg's culinary and artistic offerings.

Fashion Boutiques

Fashionistas wishing to enhance their wardrobe with stylish finds will find a choice of fashion boutiques selling the latest trends and designer labels in Bamberg. From elegant boutiques and innovative concept stores to classic department stores and vintage shops, Bamberg's bustling shopping areas have something for any fashion-conscious consumer. Here are some good choices for fashion shopping in Bamberg:

Boutique 186: This chic boutique offers a carefully curated variety of women's clothes, accessories, and footwear from top designers and rising names. Visitors can peruse racks loaded with trendy pieces, traditional basics, and statement accessories while receiving customized styling assistance from the educated staff.

Men's Fashion Bamberg: This upmarket men's boutique caters to the sartorial demands of the modern gentleman, offering a diverse selection of tailored suits, casual clothes, accessories, and footwear from leading European and worldwide brands. Visitors can browse racks of well created items, try on the latest fashions, and enjoy a personalized shopping experience based on their specific tastes and preferences.

Vintage Bazaar: Vintage Bazaar offers a handpicked range of vintage and pre-owned apparel, accessories, and homeware from the 1950s to the 1990s. Visitors can search through racks of vintage dresses, jeans, leather jackets, and other items to find one-of-a-kind pieces to give a nostalgic touch to their wardrobe.

Whether you're looking for a one-of-a-kind memento, trying out local cuisines at a lively market, or updating your wardrobe with the latest designs, Bamberg provides a broad and exciting shopping experience that will thrill visitors of all tastes and interests.

In this chapter, we've looked at Bamberg's eclectic retail environment, from charming souvenir shops and bustling markets to sophisticated designer boutiques, each with its own assortment of items and treasures to find. Whether you're looking for traditional Bavarian souvenirs, enjoying local foods at a farmers' market, or going on a shopping spree at a fashionable fashion boutique, Bamberg welcomes visitors to shop till they drop and discover a world of riches in its scenic streets and squares. So take your shopping bags and prepare to discover the vibrant shopping scene of this charming Bavarian city.

CHAPTER 11

PRACTICAL INFORMATION
FOR VISITORS

Visiting a new place can be an exciting adventure, but you must be prepared with practical facts to guarantee a smooth and comfortable journey. This chapter will address important topics such as currency and banking services, language and communication recommendations, and where to find tourist information centers in Bamberg. Whether you're a first-time visitor or a seasoned tourist, having this useful information at your fingertips will allow you to traverse Bamberg with confidence and ease.

Currency And Banking

Before you travel to Bamberg, make sure you are familiar with the local currency and banking services available in the city.

Germany's national currency is the euro (€), which is divided into 100 cents. Euro banknotes are issued in denominations of €5, €10, €20, €50, €100, €200, and €500, while coins are issued in values of 1 cent, 2 cents, 5 cents, 10 cents, 20 cents, 50 cents, €1, and €2.

Bamberg provides a variety of banking services, including currency exchange, cash withdrawals, and financial management. Numerous banks operate in the city, including big international banks like Deutsche Bank, Commerzbank, and Sparkasse, as well as smaller cooperative banks and credit unions. Most banks in Bamberg provide ATM services, which allow you to withdraw cash using your debit or credit card from worldwide networks such as Visa, Mastercard, American Express, and Maestro. ATMs are widely available around the city, notably at airports, rail stations, shopping malls, and tourist attractions.

Furthermore, many hotels, restaurants, stores, and attractions in Bamberg accept major credit cards, making it easier for visitors to make purchases and transactions without the need for cash. However, it is usually a good idea to have extra cash on hand for smaller purchases, as not all establishments accept credit cards, particularly in more distant areas or at local markets and street sellers.

Language And Communication

While German is the official language in Bamberg and throughout Germany, English is frequently understood and spoken, particularly in tourist destinations, hotels, restaurants, and stores. Most residents, particularly younger generations and those working in the tourism industry, speak English and can easily communicate with international guests.

However, knowing a few basic German phrases can improve your travel experience and allow you to engage with people on a more personal level. Here are some crucial German phrases to learn:

Guten Tag: Good day

Bitte: Please

Danke: Thank you

Entschuldigung: Excuse me

Sprechen Sie Englisch?: Do you speak English?

Wo Ist...?: Where is...?

Wie Viel Kostet Das?: How much does this cost?

Prost!: Cheers!

Making an attempt to speak a few words of German will not only demonstrate respect for the local culture, but will also make daily interactions and transactions easier throughout your stay in Bamberg.

Bamberg has good communication infrastructure, including reliable mobile phone service and internet access. Most hotels, restaurants, cafes, and public venues provide free Wi-Fi to their clients, allowing them to stay connected and share their vacation experiences with friends and family back home. International travelers can also buy prepaid SIM cards from local mobile companies including Deutsche Telekom, Vodafone, and O2, which provide reasonable data and calling plans during their stay in Bamberg.

Tourist Information Centers

Travelers seeking assistance, information, and advice during their visit to Bamberg can find various tourist information centers with pleasant personnel, maps, brochures, and other resources to help them make the most of their stay. These tourist information centers give tourists with a plethora of information on sights, events, excursions, transportation alternatives, and more, allowing them to easily explore Bamberg.

Some Of The Major Tourist Information Centers In Bamberg Are:

Bamberg Tourist Information Office: Located in the heart of the Old Town, near the Altes Rathaus (Old Town Hall), is the city's major visitor facility. You can pick up maps, brochures, and guides, book guided tours and excursions, buy souvenirs and tickets, and get individual recommendations and support from knowledgeable staff.

Bamberg Hauptbahnhof (Main Train Station) Tourist Information: For those arriving by train, the tourist information desk at Bamberg Hauptbahnhof provides easy access to tourist information services such as maps, brochures, and assistance with transportation, lodging, and sightseeing options.

Bamberg Welcome Center: Located near the Michaelisplatz, the Bamberg Welcome Center greets tourists and gives information on sights, activities, dining, shopping, and lodgings in Bamberg. The center also conducts cultural events, exhibitions, and performances throughout the year to highlight the city's rich legacy and thriving cultural environment.

These tourist information centers are manned by multilingual professionals who are glad to help you with any inquiries or concerns you may have while visiting Bamberg. Whether you need directions, suggestions for restaurants or activities, or help booking tours or lodgings, the pleasant personnel at these facilities are here to help you make the most of your time in Bamberg.

In this chapter, we addressed important practical information for travelers to Bamberg, such as currency and banking services, language and communication recommendations, and where to find tourist information centers in the city. By becoming acquainted with these crucial elements, you will be well-prepared to explore Bamberg with confidence and ease, resulting in a seamless and delightful travel experience from beginning to end. Whether you're exchanging currency, practicing a few basic German words, or seeking advice from tourist information centers, having this useful information on hand will help you make the most of your trip to this charming Bavarian city.

CHAPTER 12

HEALTH AND SAFETY TIPS

When visiting a new location, it is critical to prioritize your health and safety to ensure a stress-free and pleasurable trip. In this chapter, we will go over important health and safety considerations for visitors to Bamberg, such as emergency services, travel insurance, and health precautions to take while in the city. Staying aware and prepared allows you to reduce risks and focus on making the most of your time in Bamberg.

Emergency Services

In the event of an emergency during your stay to Bamberg, it is critical to understand how to contact emergency services quickly. Germany has a well-developed emergency response system, with experienced specialists available to help you in a variety of emergencies. Here's a breakdown of Bamberg's key emergency services:

Emergency Medical Services: If you need immediate medical assistance, dial 112 to contact the ambulance service. Trained paramedics will arrive promptly at your location and offer emergency medical care as needed. Bamberg has various hospitals and medical clinics where you can obtain treatment for a variety of ailments and injuries.

Police Services: In the event of a crime, accident, or other emergency needing police help, phone 110 to contact the local police department (Polizei). The police can assist you, investigate events, and assure your safety and security during your stay in Bamberg.

Fire And Rescue Services: To contact the fire department (Feuerwehr) in the event of an emergency such as a fire, hazardous material incident, or rescue operation, phone 112. Trained firefighters and rescue professionals will arrive swiftly to help alleviate the situation and provide assistance as needed.

Poison Control Center: To report poisoning or exposure to dangerous substances, dial 19240. Trained specialists are accessible 24 hours a day, seven days a week to provide advise and assistance with poisoning emergencies.

It is critical to have these emergency numbers saved in your phone and easily accessible during your stay in Bamberg. In addition, if you are staying at a hotel or lodging, ask about their emergency procedures and contact information in case of an emergency.

Travel Insurance

Travel insurance is an important factor for any vacation, as it provides financial security and peace of mind in the event of unanticipated incidents or emergencies. Before traveling to Bamberg, it is recommended that you get comprehensive travel insurance that covers medical expenses, trip cancellation and interruption insurance, emergency medical evacuation, and covering for lost or stolen possessions.

If you become ill or injured while on your trip, travel insurance can assist cover the costs of medical treatment, hospitalization, and emergency medical transportation. It can also compensate you for non-refundable trip fees if you have to cancel or interrupt your vacation for covered reasons including illness, injury, or natural catastrophes.

When getting travel insurance, make sure to carefully check the policy terms, coverage limitations, exclusions, and conditions to ensure that you have enough coverage for your unique trip requirements. When purchasing a travel insurance policy, consider your destination, length of stay, planned activities, and any pre-existing medical conditions.

Health Precautions

While Bamberg is a safe and inviting location for visitors, you should take the required health precautions to protect yourself and reduce the chance of illness or injury during your visit. Here are some health precautions to consider:

Stay Hydrated: Drink plenty of water, especially during hot weather or vigorous exertion, to avoid dehydration.

Maintain Good Hygiene: Wash your hands frequently with soap and water, especially before eating or handling food, after using the restroom, or after touching surfaces in public places.

Protect Against Insect Bites: If you'll be spending time outside, especially in wooded or rural areas, wear long sleeves and pants, use insect repellent with DEET or picaridin, and avoid areas with high mosquito activity, especially at dawn and dusk.

Sun Protection: Wear sunscreen with a high SPF, sunglasses, and a wide-brimmed hat to shield your skin and eyes from the sun's damaging UV rays, especially during peak hours.

Stay Active: Maintain a healthy lifestyle by staying active, eating good meals, getting enough rest, and dealing with stress during your trip.

Seek Medical Advice: If you have any pre-existing medical conditions or are concerned about your health while traveling, speak with your healthcare professional before your trip for tailored advice and recommendations.

By following these health precautions and remaining informed about emergency services and travel insurance alternatives, you can have a safe and healthy visit to Bamberg and make the most of your time seeing this lovely Bavarian city.

This chapter contains important health and safety suggestions for visitors to Bamberg, such as information on emergency services, travel insurance, and health precautions to take while in the city. By familiarizing yourself with these practical advise and being prepared, you may have a stress-free and delightful trip to Bamberg, focusing on making lasting memories and seeing everything this quaint Bavarian city has to offer.

CHAPTER 13

TRANSPORTATION WITHIN BAMBERG

Navigating a new city, such as Bamberg, may be a fascinating journey, especially when you have easy transportation alternatives available. This chapter will look at many means to move around Bamberg, including as public transportation, bicycle rentals, taxis, and ridesharing services. Whether you want to explore on foot, cycle along gorgeous trails, or take a ride to your destination, Bamberg has a variety of transportation options to meet your preferences.

Public Transportation Options

Bamberg has an efficient and dependable public transportation system, making it simple to explore the city and its surroundings. The Bamberg City Bus Company

(Stadtwerke Bamberg) operates the principal means of public transportation in Bamberg, which are buses and trams. Here's everything you need to know about public transportation choices in Bamberg:

Buses: Bamberg's bus network connects the city and its outskirts, offering easy access to major attractions, neighborhoods, and transportation hubs. Bus routes are clearly signposted, with specified stops and schedules published at each stop. Visitors can buy single-ride tickets or day passes from ticket machines at bus stops, on buses, and at select businesses.

Trams: The Bamberg Light Railway (Bamberger Straßenbahn), which serves the city center and adjacent areas, is an efficient and environmentally friendly method of transportation. Trams operate on dedicated tracks and follow predetermined itineraries, making it simple to explore the city's major thoroughfares and attractions. Tram tickets, like buses, can be purchased at ticket machines or on board the tram.

Fares And Passes: The Bamberg City Bus Company provides a variety of fare alternatives to meet varied travel demands, such as single-ride tickets, day passes, and multi-day passes.

Visitors can also purchase integrated tickets that grant them access to both buses and trams within the city limits. It is recommended that you check the current fare costs and ticket options before taking public transportation in Bamberg.

Public transportation in Bamberg is a handy and cost-effective method to experience the city and its surroundings, allowing visitors to travel comfortably and efficiently while minimizing their environmental impact.

Bicycle Rentals

Bicycle rentals are a popular alternative for individuals who want to explore Bamberg at their own speed and enjoy the freedom of the open road. Bamberg is a bicycle-friendly city with well-marked bike lanes, picturesque cycling routes, and plenty of bike parking options. Here's all you should know about renting bicycles in Bamberg:

Bike Rental Businesses: Several bike rental businesses are scattered throughout Bamberg, offering a wide range of bicycles for rent, including city bikes, mountain bikes, electric bikes (e-bikes), and tandem bikes. Rental fees are usually reasonable and vary depending on the type of bike, length of rental, and additional services such as helmet rental or bike locks.

Self-Service Bike Rentals: In addition to typical rental shops, Bamberg has self-service bike rental systems, which allow users to hire bikes directly from automated bike stations using a smartphone app or credit card. These self-service systems enable easy access to bicycles at numerous sites throughout the city, allowing users to pick up and put off bikes as they want.

Riding Routes: Bamberg has a network of attractive riding routes that weave through the city's old streets, along the River Regnitz, and into the surrounding countryside. Whether you're touring Bamberg's UNESCO World Heritage Old Town or biking through scenic vineyards and woodlands, cycling provides a unique and engaging way to enjoy the city's beauty and charm.

Bicycle rentals provide visitors to Bamberg a flexible and environmentally responsible transportation choice, allowing them to explore the city at their leisure while reaping the health advantages of cycling and lowering their carbon footprint.

Taxi And Ridesharing Services

Taxis and rideshare services are easily available in Bamberg for travelers looking for convenient, door-to-door transportation. Whether you need a fast trip to your hotel, a lift to a nearby destination, or transportation to the airport or train station, taxis and rideshare services provide an easy answer. Here's everything you need to know about taxi and ridesharing services in Bamberg:

Taxi Services: Bamberg has various taxi firms that operate across the city and nearby areas. Taxis can be hailed on the street, hired over the phone, or requested from taxi stands near prominent tourist attractions, transportation hubs, and hotels. Taxi prices are regulated by the city and usually metered based on distance traveled.

Ridesharing Services: In addition to regular taxis, ridesharing services like Uber may be accessible in Bamberg, offering on-demand transportation at competitive prices. The ridesharing app allows travelers to book trips, track their driver's whereabouts in real time, and pay for their trip electronically via a linked payment option.

Airport Transfers: Taxis and ridesharing services provide handy transportation choices for passengers arriving or departing from Bamberg's airport or train station. Many taxi firms and rideshare drivers provide airport transfer services at fixed rates or reduced pricing, making it a convenient method to get there.

Taxis and ridesharing services provide a convenient and dependable transportation alternative for travelers in Bamberg, with door-to-door service and flexible scheduling to match your travel needs.

In this chapter, we looked at the many modes of transportation accessible in Bamberg, such as public transit, bicycle rentals, and taxi and ridesharing services. Whether you prefer the ease of public transit, the freedom of cycling, or the flexibility of taxi and ridesharing services, Bamberg has a variety of transportation options to meet your preferences and travel needs. By taking use of these transit choices, you can easily navigate the city and discover everything Bamberg has to offer, from historic landmarks and cultural attractions to gorgeous countryside and lovely neighborhoods.

CHAPTER 14

ITINERARIES AND SAMPLE

PLANS

Given Bamberg's rich history, cultural legacy, and numerous attractions, planning your trip there can be both exciting and overwhelming. In this chapter, we'll present you with two sample itineraries to help you make the most of your visit to Bamberg, whether you're looking for a fast weekend vacation or a more in-depth cultural immersion experience. These itineraries are intended to provide a healthy combination of sightseeing, cultural experiences, dining, and relaxation, allowing you to see the most that Bamberg has to offer.

Weekend Getaway

For those with limited time, a weekend visit to Bamberg is the ideal way to discover the city's highlights and immerse themselves in its distinct character. Here's a recommended itinerary for an unforgettable weekend in Bamberg:

Day One: Arrival and Old Town Exploration.

Morning: Arrive in Bamberg and settle into your accommodations. Begin your day with a leisurely breakfast at a local cafe, which includes freshly brewed coffee and classic Bavarian pastries.

Late Morning: Walk around Bamberg's UNESCO World Heritage Old Town. Begin your walking tour at the historic Altes Rathaus (Old Town Hall) on the gorgeous Obere Brücke (Upper Bridge), which boasts stunning architecture and a unique setting.

Afternoon: Continue your journey of the Old Town, stopping by ancient sites such as the Bamberg Cathedral (Bamberger Dom), the Neue Residenz (New Residence), and the Altenburg Castle. Take a walk through the picturesque tiny streets and alleyways, uncovering hidden jewels, quaint boutiques, and comfortable cafes along the route.

Evening: Dine at a traditional Franconian restaurant and sample regional specialties including Schäufele (roast pork shoulder), Bratwurst (grilled sausages), and Kartoffelsalat (potato salad). After dinner, enjoy a leisurely evening stroll along the River Regnitz to soak up the wonderful ambiance of Bamberg at night.

Day Two: Cultural Exploration, Beer Tasting

Morning: Begin your day by visiting one of Bamberg's prestigious museums or art galleries, such as the Bamberg State Library, the Bamberg Natural History Museum, or the E. T.A. Hoffmann Haus. Immerse yourself in the city's vibrant cultural heritage and discover its interesting history and traditions.

Late Morning: Visit one of Bamberg's historic breweries for a guided tour and beer tasting. Learn about the brewing process, the various beer styles produced in Bamberg, and the city's long-standing brewing traditions. Sample a selection of local beers, including the well-known Rauchbier (smoked beer), and enjoy the flavors of Bamberg's craft beer scene.

Afternoon: After the brewery tour, take a scenic boat excursion down the Regnitz River to see panoramic views of Bamberg's cityscape and landmarks from the river. Alternatively, rent a bicycle and tour the city's surrounding countryside, biking along gorgeous bike trails and through lush green landscapes.

Evening: Wrap up your weekend break with a wonderful dinner at a typical beer garden or snug pub, where hearty Bavarian dishes are matched with local beers. Raise a toast to your stay in Bamberg and cherish the memories of your weekend journey in this delightful Bavarian city.

Cultural Immersion

For those wanting a more in-depth cultural immersion experience, Bamberg provides numerous possibilities to learn about its rich history, customs, and traditions. Here's a recommended agenda for a cultural immersion trip in Bamberg:

Day One: Historical landmarks and architectural wonders.

Morning: Start your cultural immersion experience with a guided walking tour of Bamberg's UNESCO World Heritage Old Town. Explore the city's ancient landmarks, such as the Bamberg Cathedral, the Altes Rathaus (Old Town Hall), and the charming Fishermen's Quarter. Discover Bamberg's medieval beginnings, its significance as a hub of ecclesiastical power, and its distinctive architectural styles.

Late Morning: Visit the Bamberg State Library, which has a large collection of rare books, manuscripts, and relics dating back centuries. Admire the library's spectacular Baroque architecture and exquisite interior design, which includes elegant ceilings, rich woodwork, and detailed murals.

Afternoon: Explore Bamberg's rich artistic heritage at the E. T. A. Hoffmann Haus was the former home of the famed German author, composer, and artist. Explore the museum's displays on Hoffmann's life and work, which include his well-known stories of mystery, fantasy, and the occult.

Evening: Take in a classical music concert or theatrical production at one of Bamberg's prestigious cultural institutions, such as the Konzerthalle Bamberg or the ETA Hoffmann Theater. Immerse yourself in the city's thriving cultural scene and witness the thrill of live performance in a historic setting.

Day Two: Art, Music, and Culinary Delights

Morning: Begin your day with a visit to the Bamberg Natural History Museum, located in the old Franciscan Monastery.

Explore the museum's extensive collections of flora, fauna, fossils, and minerals to learn about Franconian natural history.

Late Morning: Enjoy a leisurely stroll around Bamberg's magnificent parks and gardens, such as Hain Park or the Rose Garden, admiring the scenic vistas and bright floral displays. Pause for a leisurely picnic lunch amidst nature, savoring local foods and taking in the peaceful atmosphere.

Afternoon: Immerse yourself in Bamberg's culinary heritage by taking a hands-on cooking lesson or tour. You'll learn how to make authentic Bavarian meals with fresh, locally sourced ingredients. Learn the secrets of Franconian cuisine from skilled chefs and enjoy a delectable feast of regional favorites.

Evening: Wrap up your cultural immersion tour with a visit to one of Bamberg's renowned art galleries or exhibitions, which feature works by local and international artists. Reflect on your cultural experiences while enjoying a leisurely supper at a gourmet restaurant, relishing the flavors of Bamberg's culinary scene and raising a toast to the city's rich cultural legacy.

In this chapter, we've offered two sample itineraries to help you plan your trip to Bamberg, whether you're searching for a fast weekend vacation or a more in-depth cultural experience. From visiting historical landmarks and architectural wonders to indulging in gastronomic pleasures and attending cultural events, these itineraries provide a diverse range of activities to fit any traveler's interests and tastes. By following these suggested itineraries or tailoring them to your preferences, you can make the most of your stay in Bamberg and create wonderful memories.

Outdoor Adventure

Outdoor enthusiasts and nature lovers will find a wealth of fascinating outdoor activities in Bamberg's gorgeous natural environments. Whether you're looking for thrilling experiences or relaxing outdoor activities, Bamberg has something for everyone. Here's a recommended itinerary for an unforgettable outdoor experience in Bamberg.

Day One: Active Exploration and Scenic Views

Morning: Begin your day with an exhilarating climb to Altenburg Castle, which sits atop one of Bamberg's seven hills. Scenic routes wind through lush forests and meadows, providing panoramic views of the city and surrounding area. Explore the castle remains and discover its fascinating history as a historic fortress overlooking Bamberg.

Late Morning: Depart from Altenburg Castle and continue your outdoor adventure with a bike trip along the scenic River Regnitz. Rent a bicycle from a local rental shop and ride along designated bike lanes that wind past picturesque villages, vineyards, and countryside scenery. Stop for a picnic lunch by the riverbank and enjoy the calm of nature.

Afternoon: Go kayaking or canoeing along the calm waters of the Regnitz River. Paddle at your own pace, discovering secret coves, wildlife habitats, and historical sites along the riverbank. Keep a look out for native bird species including herons, kingfishers, and ducks that live along the river.

Evening: Wrap up your day of outdoor discovery with a sunset hike to Michaelsberg Abbey, another stunning vantage point with panoramic views of Bamberg and the surrounding area. Capture the golden hues of the setting sun against the backdrop of the city's historic skyline before returning to the center.

Day Two: Family-Friendly Fun and Adventure

Morning: Begin your family-friendly excursion by visiting the Bamberg Zoo, which is home to a wide assortment of animals from around the world. Explore the zoo's themed exhibits, which include African savannas, Asian rainforests, and European woodlands, and see exotic animals including lions, giraffes, elephants, and monkeys.

Late Morning: Visit Erba Island, a scenic leisure area on the River Regnitz, for a morning of outdoor activities and relaxation. Allow the kids to burn off energy on the island's playgrounds and sports areas, or rent pedal boats and paddle around the quiet lake. Pack a picnic lunch and enjoy a gorgeous outdoor supper among the lush vegetation.

Afternoon: Continue your family-friendly journey by visiting Bambados, Bamberg's premier leisure and water park. Splash and play in the park's indoor and outdoor pools, whirlpools, and water slides, or unwind in the sauna and spa for some much-needed rest and relaxation.

Evening: Finish off your family-friendly vacation with a classic Bavarian meal at a comfortable restaurant or beer garden, where you can eat robust foods like Schnitzel,

Bratwurst, and Spaetzle. Raise a drink to your unforgettable family experience in Bamberg, and cherish the memories you made together in this delightful Bavarian city.

Family-Friendly Trip

Traveling with your family can be a pleasant experience, especially when you visit a welcoming and family-friendly place like Bamberg. Bamberg has a wide range of activities for guests of all ages, including interactive museums and outdoor excursions, cultural attractions, and culinary pleasures. Here's a recommended agenda for a memorable family trip to Bamberg:

Day One: Exploring Bamberg's Family Attractions

Morning: Begin the day by visiting the Franconian Brewery Museum, where families can learn about the craft of producing beer and the history of Bamberg's brewing traditions. Visitors of all ages can learn about the brewing process through interactive exhibitions, hands-on activities, and brewing demonstrations.

Late Morning: Visit the Bamberg State Library, where families can embark on a literary journey through the library's extensive collection of books, manuscripts, and historical objects. Participate in family-friendly guided tours, storytelling sessions, and craft workshops based on classic stories and literary themes.

Afternoon: Treat the youngsters to an afternoon of fun and excitement at the Playmobil FunPark, which is only a short drive from Bamberg. Let their imaginations run free as they explore themed play areas, interactive displays, and thrilling rides inspired by popular Playmobil toy sets. Don't forget to bring a picnic lunch to enjoy in the park's gorgeous outdoor areas.

Evening: End the day with a leisurely stroll through Bamberg's Old Town, where families may explore the city's historic landmarks, lovely architecture, and vibrant street scenes. Stop for dinner at a family-friendly restaurant or cafe and eat excellent local favorites and Bavarian delicacies.

Day Two: Outdoor Activities and Nature Exploration.

Morning: Spend the morning touring Bamberg's lovely parks and green spaces, such as Hain Park and the Rose Garden. Allow the youngsters to run and play in the lush gardens, scenic walking routes, and colorful flower beds, or have a relaxing family picnic surrounded by nature's beauty.

Late Morning: Visit the Bamberg Zoo, where families may see a variety of animals from throughout the world in themed displays and realistic settings. Participate in educational animal feedings, interactive keeper talks, and hands-on interactions with friendly zoo animals.

Afternoon: Continue your outdoor experiences by visiting Erba Island, a popular recreation spot on the River Regnitz. Rent a bicycle, pedal boat, or inline skates to explore the island's scenic pathways, playgrounds, and sports fields, or simply relax and enjoy the sunshine by the river.

Evening: Wrap up your family-friendly trip with a wonderful meal in a classic Bavarian restaurant or beer garden, where you can eat hearty foods and local delicacies while reminiscing about your adventures in Bamberg. Raise a toast to family fun and togetherness in this picturesque Bavarian city.

In this chapter, we've included two sample itineraries for people considering a trip to Bamberg, whether they want an outdoor adventure or a family vacation. These itineraries offer a wide range of activities to suit any traveler's interests and tastes, from hiking to castles and kayaking down rivers to visiting zoos and theme parks. By following these suggested plans or tailoring them to your preferences, you may create wonderful memories and experiences in Bamberg that the entire family will treasure for years to come.

Budget Travel

Traveling on a budget does not imply compromising on experiences. Bamberg has numerous possibilities for budget-conscious travelers to visit its sites, sample its cuisine, and immerse themselves in its culture without breaking the bank. Here's a budget-friendly schedule for exploring Bamberg:

Day One: Exploring Bamberg's Free Attractions

Morning: Begin your day with a self-guided walking tour of Bamberg's Old Town, which has many of the city's most renowned buildings and historic attractions. Explore the cobblestone alleys, attractive lanes, and picturesque squares, including the Altes Rathaus (Old Town Hall), Bamberg Cathedral, and the quaint Fishermen's Quarter.

Late Morning: Visit one of Bamberg's numerous museums and cultural institutions, which provide free or subsidized admission on certain days. The options include the Bamberg State Library, the Franconian Brewery Museum, and the E. T. A. Hoffmann Haus, where visitors can learn about Bamberg's literary and cultural heritage.

Afternoon: Have a low-cost picnic lunch in one of Bamberg's picturesque parks or green areas, such as Hain Park or the Rose Garden. Pick up fresh produce, bread, and cheese at a local market or bakery, then locate a nice area to relax and dine al fresco surrounded by nature's beauty.

Evening: Take advantage of Bamberg's lively street food scene and reasonably priced eating options. Try local favorites like Bratwurst (grilled sausages), Kartoffelsalat (potato salad), and Brotzeit (bread and cold meats) at food stalls, market vendors, or informal cafés that serve traditional Bavarian fare.

Day Two: Outdoor Adventures and Cultural Discovery

Morning: Begin your day with a lovely trek or bike ride along the River Regnitz, taking in Bamberg's beautiful countryside and surrounding surroundings. Pack a small breakfast or snacks to eat on the move, and marvel at nature's grandeur as you travel along gorgeous trails and walkways.

Late Morning: Stop by one of Bamberg's free or low-cost cultural sites, such as the Bamberg Natural History Museum or Michaelsberg Abbey. Discover the region's natural history, plants, and fauna, or explore the abbey's ancient grounds and panoramic views over the city.

Afternoon: Explore Bamberg's colorful neighborhoods and local markets, where you may find inexpensive souvenirs, handcrafted crafts, and unusual presents. Explore hidden gems and off-the-beaten-path sites to discover the city's genuine charm and local flavor.

Evening: Finish your budget-friendly excursion with a leisurely stroll along the River Regnitz or through Bamberg's Old Town, taking in the city's charming ambiance and historic beauty. Grab a drink at a nice pub or beer garden to unwind after a day of exploring without breaking the budget.

Solo Traveler's Guide

Traveling solo to Bamberg provides a unique opportunity to explore the city at your own leisure, immerse yourself in its culture, and meet other travelers along the route. Here is a suggested schedule for single travelers who want to enjoy the finest of Bamberg on their own:

Day One: Solo Exploration and Cultural Discovery.

Morning: Begin your solo journey with a self-guided walking tour of Bamberg's Old Town, where you may explore ancient sites, picturesque lanes, and hidden treasures at your own pace. Take some time to walk off the usual path, visit local cafés and businesses, and capture the city's beauty with your own lens.

Late Morning: Visit one of Bamberg's museums or cultural institutions to learn about the city's rich history, art, and tradition. Choose audio-guided tours or interactive exhibitions that let you to study and explore at your own pace, providing insights into Bamberg's intriguing history and cultural relevance.

Afternoon: Have a leisurely lunch at a comfortable cafe or restaurant, where you may sample traditional Bavarian foods and regional delicacies. Take advantage of the opportunity to chat with locals or fellow travelers while enjoying a delicious dinner, swapping tales, recommendations, and travel ideas.

Evening: Enjoy a cultural event or live performance in one of Bamberg's theaters, symphony halls, or performance venues. Immerse yourself in the city's dynamic arts scene, where you may enjoy music, theater, dance, and opera in a historic setting that exemplifies Bamberg's cultural depth and diversity.

Day Two: Outdoor Adventures and Solo Reflection

Morning: Begin your day with an early morning stroll along the River Regnitz or through Bamberg's picturesque parks and gardens, where you can find serenity among nature's majesty. Take some time to contemplate, meditate, or simply relax as you prepare for another day of exploring.

Late Morning: Go on a solo excursion to one of Bamberg's local attractions or day trip destinations, such as the Franconian Wine Country or nearby castle ruins. Take a scenic train journey or rent a bicycle to explore the countryside, discovering hidden gems and beautiful scenery along the way.

Afternoon: Return to Bamberg and spend your day exploring the city's diverse neighborhoods, local markets, and craft stores. Spend some time shopping for souvenirs, handcrafted crafts, or one-of-a-kind things to remember your solo adventure and experiences in Bamberg.

Evening: End your solo excursion with a memorable dinner at a cozy restaurant or beer garden, where you may celebrate your independence and the adventures you had in Bamberg. As you bid farewell to this picturesque Bavarian city, think about the memories made, the lessons learned, and the connections formed.

In this chapter, we've included two sample itineraries to appeal to various types of visitors to Bamberg. Whether you're seeing the city on a budget or going on a solo adventure, these itineraries have a variety of activities and experiences to fit your tastes and interests. By following these suggested plans or tailoring them to your specific needs, you may create wonderful memories and experiences in Bamberg that are unique to your travel style and tastes

Romantic Getaways

Bamberg's stunning environment, historic charm, and romantic atmosphere make it an ideal location for a romantic weekend with your sweetheart. Whether you're celebrating a special event or simply looking for quality time together, Bamberg has a plethora of romantic adventures to enjoy. Here's a suggested agenda for an unforgettable romantic break in Bamberg:

Day One: Romance in Bamberg's Old Town.

Early Morning: Start your romantic holiday with a relaxing breakfast at a nice cafe or bakery in Bamberg's Old Town. Enjoy freshly made pastries, artisanal bread, and locally roasted coffee as you begin your day with a loved one.

Late Morning: Take a romantic stroll around Bamberg's UNESCO World Heritage-listed Old Town with your spouse. Explore the small cobblestone alleys, medieval squares, and beautiful lanes, pausing to admire architectural marvels like the Altes Rathaus (Old Town Hall) and Bamberg Cathedral.

Afternoon: Take a magnificent boat tour over the calm waters of the River Regnitz, savoring panoramic views of Bamberg's cityscape and landmarks from the river. Choose a private boat excursion or a shared cruise to spend time with your sweetheart and experience a romantic moment surrounded by nature's splendor.

Evening: Enjoy a romantic candlelit dinner at one of Bamberg's top restaurants, where you can appreciate gourmet cuisine and superb wines in an intimate environment. Choose a restaurant with a beautiful view or a snug corner table, and toast your love with a glass of sparkling champagne.

Day Two: Romantic escapes and cultural delights.

Morning: Begin the day by visiting one of Bamberg's charming gardens or parks, such as the Rose Garden or the Hain Park. Take a leisurely stroll through blossoming flowers, lush vegetation, and quiet ponds, soaking up the beauty of nature and the tranquility of your surroundings.

Late Morning: Tour Bamberg's cultural attractions with your spouse, including museums, galleries, and historic sites that reflect the city's rich tradition and artistic legacy. Choose exhibits and events that are relevant to your interests as a pair, such as art, history, or literature.

Afternoon: Enjoy a romantic wine tasting experience at one of Bamberg's local vineyards or wine bars, where you may try a selection of Franconian wines while learning about the region's winemaking traditions. Enjoy every sip as you explore new flavors and fragrances together.

Evening: Wrap up your romantic weekend with a moonlit walk along the River Regnitz or through Bamberg's Old Town, where you can see the city's illuminated landmarks and bridges. Find a quiet area to sit and enjoy the serene atmosphere, gazing up at the starry sky and remembering the moments you enjoyed with your loved one.

In this chapter, we've included an example schedule for couples planning a romantic holiday to Bamberg. These experiences, which range from leisurely strolls around the Old Town to breathtaking boat excursions along the river and private meals at fine restaurants, are intended to help you make amazing memories and celebrate your love in Bamberg's charming surroundings. By following this suggested itinerary or tailoring it to your tastes, you can create the ideal romantic getaway based on your unique relationship and shared interests.

CHAPTER 15

HIDDEN GEMS AND OFF-THE-BEATEN-PATH ATTRACTIONS

Bamberg, with its rich history and cultural legacy, has numerous hidden jewels and off-the-beaten-path sites that adventurous travelers can uncover. Away from the bustling tourist highlights, these lesser-known locations provide unique experiences and insights into the city's charm and character. In this chapter, we'll learn about some of Bamberg's best-kept secrets, including secret gardens, offbeat museums, and local art pieces that contribute to the city's attractiveness.

Secret Garden And Courtyard

While Bamberg's Old Town is known for its medieval architecture and historic attractions, it also contains charming secret gardens and calm courtyards hidden behind ancient walls and underground passages. These hidden oases provide a calm respite from the rush and bustle of city life, enticing tourists to relax amidst lush vegetation and vibrant blossoms. Here are a few secret gardens and courtyards to explore:

Rose Garden: The Rose Garden, located atop Michaelsberg Hill, provides breathtaking panoramic views of Bamberg's Old Town and surrounding countryside. Tucked away behind Michaelsberg Abbey, this hidden gem boasts a wide collection of roses in all colors and aromas, making it ideal for a romantic stroll or solitary contemplation.

Klein Venedig: Klein Venedig, which translates to "Little Venice," is a hidden gem on the banks of the Regnitz River. This charming district is distinguished by a row of colorful fishermen's houses with overhanging balconies that evoke the canals of Venice. Explore the narrow cobblestone alleyways and quiet waterfront promenades, stopping at hidden cafes and boutique shops along the route.

Bamberg Cathedral Cloister: Enter the quiet cloister of Bamberg Cathedral to find a hidden haven of solitude and serenity. Admire the exquisite stone carvings, arches, and lush foliage that surround this secret courtyard, and take in the timeless beauty of this hallowed area away from the masses.

Quirky Museums

Aside from standard museums and cultural institutions, Bamberg is home to a number of quirky and unconventional museums that provide distinct perspectives on the city's history, culture, and legacy. These unique museums, with their unusual collections and interactive exhibits, are sure to stimulate the interest of adventurous tourists. Here are a few interesting museums to include on your itinerary:

Bicycle Museum Bamberg: Housed in a historic brewery building, the Bicycle Museum Bamberg commemorates the history and evolution of cycling with an intriguing collection of vintage bicycles, memorabilia, and artifacts. Discover the progression of bicycle design, from penny-farthings to modern mountain bikes, and learn about Bamberg's cycling culture and legacy.

Puppenmuseum (Doll Museum): Located in the heart of Bamberg's Old Town, the Puppenmuseum is a hidden treasure dedicated to the art and history of dollmaking. Discover a unique collection of antique dolls, puppets, and marionettes from many countries and time periods, as well as the workmanship and skills that went into making these beloved childhood toys.

Fachwerkhaus Museum (Half-Timbered House Museum): Travel back in time and discover Bamberg's rich architectural legacy at the Fachwerkhaus Museum. This unique museum, housed in a wonderfully preserved half-timbered building, demonstrates the construction techniques and craftsmanship utilized in traditional timber-framed houses, providing insights into Bamberg's medieval past.

Local Art Installations

In addition to its historic sites and cultural attractions, Bamberg has a thriving arts scene, with a range of local art installations and creative spaces showcasing the city's modern artistic talents. From street art and sculptures to outdoor exhibitions, these hidden gems modernize Bamberg's ancient setting. Here are some local art projects to check out:

Street Art Tour: Take a self-guided tour of Bamberg's lively street art culture to see the colorful murals, graffiti, and urban art that grace the city's walls, alleys, and public areas. From colorful artwork to thought-provoking themes, each mural tells a narrative and injects some creativity into Bamberg's streets.

Kunstbahnsteig (Art Platform): Located in Bamberg's central train station, the Kunstbahnsteig is a cutting-edge art facility that exhibits contemporary art installations by local and international artists. Explore the platform's ever-changing exhibitions and installations, which include sculptures, installations, multimedia, and interactive art projects.

Kunstmeile (Art Mile): Follow Bamberg's "Kunstmeile," or Art Mile, a designated route that takes tourists past a collection of outdoor art works and sculptures located around the city. These public artworks, which range from abstract sculptures to avant-garde installations, bring a new touch to Bamberg's old streets and squares.

In this chapter, we've looked at Bamberg's hidden gems and off-the-beaten-path attractions, including secret gardens, quirky museums, and local art installations that add to the city's allure. By getting off the tourist track and discovering these lesser-known attractions, visitors can gain new perspectives and experiences that reveal Bamberg's hidden beauty and charm. Whether you're looking for peace and quiet amidst beautiful vegetation, unique cultural experiences, or modern artistic manifestations, these hidden gems provide a glimpse into the heart and soul of this enchanting Bavarian city.

CHAPTER 16

RELIGIOUS SITES IN BAMBERG

Bamberg's religious past is inextricably linked to its history and culture, as evidenced by the numerous splendid cathedrals, abbeys, and synagogues that dot the city skyline. In this chapter, we'll visit some of the city's most renowned religious sites, each providing an insight into Bamberg's spiritual history and architectural magnificence.

Bamberg Cathedral

Bamberg Cathedral, commonly known as Bamberger Dom, is the city's most recognizable religious landmark. Built in the 11th century, this towering Romanesque cathedral is dedicated to St. Peter and St. George and houses the Archbishop of Bamberg. Its massive twin towers dominate the skyline, inviting tourists to discover its rich history and stunning architecture.

History: Emperor Henry II and his wife, Empress Kunigunde, commissioned the construction of Bamberg Cathedral in 1004. The cathedral has been renovated and expanded several times over the years, resulting in its current blend of Romanesque, Gothic, and Baroque characteristics.

Architecture: Bamberg Cathedral's exterior features a magnificent red sandstone facade, complex sculptures, and artistic reliefs of biblical themes and saints. The interior boasts soaring vaulted ceilings, majestic arches, and an abundance of medieval artwork, including the legendary Bamberg Rider, a statue thought to symbolize Emperor Henry II.

Highlights: Don't miss Bamberg Cathedral's four majestic towers, which provide panoramic views of the city and surrounding countryside. Explore the interior chapels, crypts, and cloisters, admiring the spectacular stained glass windows, altarpieces, and religious items stored inside.

Michaelsberg Abbey

Michaelsberg Abbey, located atop Michaelsberg Hill and overlooks the Old Town, is another important religious landmark in Bamberg. Benedictine monks founded the abbey in the 12th century, and it has functioned as a center of religious and cultural life for centuries, influencing Bamberg's spiritual and intellectual history.

History: In 1015, Emperor Henry II and his wife, Empress Kunigunde, founded Michaelsberg Abbey as a Benedictine monastery. Over time, the abbey grew into a renowned center of study, art, and spirituality in the region.

Architecture: The abbey's Romanesque church, with its characteristic twin towers and exquisite exterior, is a medieval masterpiece. Inside, visitors may see gorgeous murals, complex stucco work, a magnificent Baroque high altar, and the tombs of Emperor Henry II and Empress Kunigunde.

Attractions: Visit the abbey's museum, library, and cloister, which house an extensive collection of religious items, manuscripts, and works of art going back to the Middle Ages. Don't miss the panoramic views of Bamberg from the abbey's high elevation, which provide a stunning setting for contemplation and introspection.

Churches And Synagogues

In addition to Bamberg Cathedral and Michaelsberg Abbey, the city has other churches and synagogues, each with its own history and architectural style.

St. Martin's Church: St. Martin's Church, which dates back to the 12th century, is one of Bamberg's oldest churches, with Romanesque architecture and beautiful murals.

St. Jakob's Church: This Gothic church boasts an intricately carved choir screen, breathtaking stained glass windows, and a tall spire that dominates the horizon.

Old Synagogue: Constructed in the nineteenth century, the Old Synagogue is a testimony to Bamberg's Jewish legacy, with a remarkable Moorish Revival architecture.

New Synagogue: Built in the early twentieth century, the New Synagogue is an architectural marvel with its Art Nouveau exterior and Byzantine-style dome.

In this chapter, we looked at some of Bamberg's most important religious sites, such as Bamberg Cathedral, Michaelsberg Abbey, and a variety of churches and synagogues that reflect the city's rich spiritual legacy. Whether you're admiring the majesty of a medieval cathedral, visiting the tranquil cloisters of an abbey, or finding the rich symbolism of a historic synagogue, these religious sites provide a peek into Bamberg's past and present as a center of faith, culture, and community.

CHAPTER 17

DINING ETIQUETTE AND CUSTOMS

Dining in Bamberg is more than just savoring wonderful food; it is also an opportunity to learn about local culture and customs. Understanding the nuances of eating etiquette can improve your culinary experiences and ensure a pleasurable supper. In this chapter, we'll look into Bamberg's dining customs and how to manage them with grace and respect.

Tipping Practices

Tipping in Bamberg is similar to that in other regions of Germany, however it is not as common or anticipated as in other nations. Here is a guide about tipping habits in Bamberg.

Restaurants: It is common to tip for good service in restaurants, but it is not required. If you are pleased with the service, leave a tip of 5-10% of the entire amount. When you pay the bill, you can leave the tip in cash on the table, or you can tell the waitress how much you want to pay, including the tip.

Cafes And Bars: Tipping in cafes and bars is less usual than in restaurants, however rounding up the bill or giving a modest tip for excellent service is appreciated. You can leave the tip on the table or hand it over to the server when you pay.

Taxi Drivers: It is common to round up the fare to the closest euro or leave a little tip for taxi drivers in Bamberg. If the service was extraordinary, you may tip more generously, but it is not expected.

Reservation Etiquette

Making reservations at restaurants in Bamberg is often recommended, especially at popular or high-end locations, to secure a table upon arrival. Here are some suggestions on reservation etiquette.

Make Reservations In Advance: It's a good idea to make reservations ahead of time, especially for dinner or on weekends when restaurants are typically busy. You can normally make reservations online, over the phone, or through a reservation platform.

Arriving On Time: If you've made a reservation, make sure to come on time or slightly early. If you are running late, it is polite to phone the restaurant and notify them, as a late arrival can inconvenience other diners and disturb the business's schedule.

Group Reservations: If you're dining with a large group, you should make a reservation in advance to guarantee that the restaurant can accommodate your party. Some restaurants may require a deposit or a set menu for large groups, so make sure to ask about any specific needs when making your reservation.

Cultural Dining Traditions

Dining in Bamberg is steeped in history, with specific customs and etiquette reflecting the city's cultural background. Below are some cultural dining practices to be mindful of:

Paying The Bill: In Bamberg, the bill is usually brought to the table after you've finished your meal. Unlike in some countries, where the server may bring the bill without prompting, it is usual to request the bill ("die Rechnung, bitte") when you are ready to pay.

Greeting And Seating: When entering a restaurant or dining institution, it is traditional to greet the host or server with a polite "Guten Tag" (Good day) or "Guten Abend" (Good evening) before asking for a table. If you're not sure whether to seat yourself or wait to be seated, ask the host for help.

Table Manners: In Bamberg, as in much of Germany, good table manners are extremely important. It is generally courteous to keep your hands visible on the table while eating, refrain from speaking with your mouth full, and avoid gesturing or pointing with your utensils. In addition, it is usual to say "Guten Appetit" (Enjoy your meal) before commencing your meal and "Danke" (Thank you) when the waitress brings your food or clears your plates.

In this chapter, we looked into Bamberg dining etiquette and customs, including tipping standards, reservation etiquette, and cultural eating traditions. Understanding and observing these conventions allows you to improve your dining experiences in Bamberg and enjoy local cuisine with confidence and respect for the city's cultural heritage. Whether you're dining in a tiny cafe or a Michelin-starred restaurant, following these etiquette rules will ensure a memorable and comfortable lunch in Bamberg.

CHAPTER 18

CULTURAL ETIQUETTE AND RESPECTFUL BEHAVIOR

Understanding and observing cultural etiquette is vital when visiting Bamberg since it allows for seamless interactions with locals while also fostering mutual respect and understanding. This chapter will provide insights into Bamberg's cultural norms and expectations, including dress code requirements, greeting customs, and photography etiquette, allowing you to negotiate social settings with elegance and compassion.

Dress Code Guidelines

Bamberg is a city with a rich cultural background, therefore wearing appropriately demonstrates respect for its traditions and customs. While Bamberg is typically a calm and casual city, there are some events and locations where a more formal dress code is expected. Below are some dress code standards to bear in mind:

Casual Wear: Casual wear is appropriate for everyday activities such as touring, dining at casual restaurants, and visiting the city's attractions. Choose comfortable clothing and footwear, particularly if you plan to perform a lot of walking or outdoor activities.

Smart Casual: Smart casual clothes is ideal for more formal settings, such as dinner at luxury restaurants or cultural activities. This usually entails wearing neat, well-fitting attire, such as slacks or a skirt, with a collared shirt or blouse.

Formal Wear: For important occasions such as concerts, theatrical plays, or religious ceremonies, formal wear may be necessary. Men normally wear a suit and tie, while ladies wear a dress or formal clothing. If you're unsure about the dress code, please double-check it ahead of time.

Modesty: Dress modestly in religious contexts like churches or synagogues to show respect for the sacred area. This includes avoiding attire that is overly exposing or provocative, such as shorts, tank tops, or miniskirts.

Greeting Customs

Greetings are vital in Bamberg's social interactions, as they convey respect and civility to others. Understanding local greeting customs can help you make a good first impression, whether you're meeting someone for the first time or welcoming an acquaintance. Here are some common greeting traditions in Bamberg:

Handshakes: Handshakes are the most usual way to greet in Bamberg, particularly in professional or business settings. When shaking hands, keep eye contact and use a solid but not overly forceful grasp. In more informal contexts, such as social gatherings or among friends, a handshake may be followed with a smile or a head nod.

Greetings: When meeting someone for the first time, it is usual to greet them politely with "Guten Tag" (Good day) or "Guten Abend" (Good evening), followed by their title and last name, if relevant. As an example, "Guten Tag, Herr Müller" (Good day, Mr. Müller) or "Guten Abend, Frau Schmidt" (Good evening, Mrs. Schmidt).

Kissing On The Cheek: In casual settings or among close friends and family, cheek kissing may be used as a greeting.

However, you must follow the other person's lead and avoid initiating physical contact unless they do so first.

Photography Etiquette

Given its scenic beauty and historic landmarks, Bamberg is a favorite destination for photographers. However, photographic etiquette must be followed in order to respect the privacy and rights of others, particularly in public places and cultural institutions. Here are some photography etiquette rules to follow:

Request Permission: Before photographing someone, especially strangers, it is polite to ask for permission first. This is especially significant in cultural or religious settings, where photography may be prohibited or deemed intrusive.

Follow No-Photography Signs: Many museums, churches, and cultural places in Bamberg have designated areas where photography is not permitted. Always obey these signs and avoid snapping photos in restricted areas, as this can interrupt other visitors and violate the establishment's policies.

Be Considerate Of others: When shooting photos in crowded or busy areas, keep other visitors in mind and avoid blocking routes or obstructing vistas. Wait for the right moment to take your shot without disturbing people, and constantly be mindful of your surroundings.

Avoid Flash Photography: Avoid using flash photography in museums, galleries, and historic buildings since it might damage delicate artworks and antiques. Whenever possible, turn off your camera or smartphone's flash and take shots in natural or ambient light.

In this chapter, we looked at cultural etiquette and courteous behavior in Bamberg, including dress code rules, greeting customs, and photography etiquette. Understanding and following these cultural norms allows you to handle social interactions with confidence and respect, creating strong relationships with locals and improving your entire experience in Bamberg. Whether you're visiting historic sites, dining at local eateries, or meeting new people, maintaining cultural etiquette shows you care for Bamberg's legacy and traditions.

CHAPTER 19

SUSTAINABLE TOURISM
PRACTICES

Sustainable tourism is critical for protecting Bamberg's natural and cultural heritage while reducing harmful environmental and social impacts. In this chapter, we will look at several sustainable tourism activities, like as eco-friendly projects, responsible travel suggestions, and methods to support local communities, to ensure that visitors may enjoy Bamberg's beauty and charm for future generations.

Environmentally Friendly Initiatives

Bamberg is dedicated to fostering sustainability and environmental conservation through a variety of eco-friendly programs. From green transit choices to energy-efficient practices, the city is working to lessen its environmental impact and safeguard its natural resources. Here are some examples of environmentally friendly efforts in Bamberg:

Public Transit: Bamberg has a large network of public transit, including buses and trams, which allows visitors to explore the city without relying on their own vehicles. Tourists who use public transportation instead of driving can cut carbon emissions and traffic congestion in the city core.

Bicycle-Friendly Infrastructure: With its flat topography and well-kept bike routes, Bamberg is a cyclist's dream. Many residents and visitors choose to bike around the city, lowering their carbon footprint and enjoying a more environmentally friendly means of transportation. Visitors can explore Bamberg on two wheels by renting bicycles from a variety of rental shops or using bike-sharing programs.

Waste Reduction Programs: Bamberg aggressively supports waste reduction and recycling through its extensive waste management programs. Visitors may help these efforts by disposing of rubbish ethically, recycling whenever possible, and avoiding single-use plastic products. Many hotels, restaurants, and attractions also provide recycling programs and encourage tourists to reduce their environmental impact.

Renewable Energy Sources: To reduce dependency on fossil fuels and encourage renewable energy, Bamberg has invested in solar panels, wind turbines, and other environmentally friendly energy sources. Visitors may help these projects by booking eco-friendly lodgings that stress energy efficiency and sustainability.

Responsible Travel Tips

Responsible travel is critical for reducing negative effects on locations and encouraging sustainable tourism practices. As a visitor to Bamberg, there are numerous methods to reduce your environmental impact and contribute to the local community:

Reduce, Reuse, And Recycle: Practice responsible waste management by limiting your use of single-use plastics, reusing goods whenever possible, and recycling materials in accordance with local regulations. Bring a reusable water bottle, shopping bag, and cutlery to reduce trash on your trip.

Conserve Water And Energy: Be cautious of your water and energy consumption while in Bamberg. To reduce your environmental impact, take shorter showers and turn off lights and appliances when not in use.

Respect Nature And Wildlife: When visiting Bamberg's natural areas, like as parks, rivers, and forests, be respectful of wildlife habitats and follow local wildlife protection legislation. To maintain the beauty of natural spaces for future generations, do not disturb animals or damage vegetation, and leave them as you found them.

Support Sustainable Businesses: Select lodgings, restaurants, and tour operators who value sustainability and responsible tourist practices. Look for eco-certifications like Green Key or Travelife, which demonstrate a dedication to environmental management and community engagement.

Supporting Local Communities

Supporting local communities is critical for promoting economic development and conserving Bamberg's cultural legacy. Visitors may help the community develop and thrive by supporting locally owned businesses, participating in cultural activities, and interacting with inhabitants. Here are several methods to support the local communities in Bamberg.

Shop Local: Buy souvenirs, presents, and handicrafts from local craftsmen, marketplaces, and stores to help small businesses and craftspeople. Look for products that highlight Bamberg's cultural past, such as traditional crafts, artisanal delicacies, and locally produced items.

Dine At Local Restaurants: Dining at locally owned restaurants and cafes allows you to enjoy traditional Bavarian cuisine while also supporting local farmers and producers. Choose eateries that use locally produced products and provide dishes crafted with fresh food.

Take Part In Cultural Experiences: Immerse yourself in Bamberg's lively culture and tradition by visiting festivals, events, and cultural shows. Attending performances and purchasing their artwork or stuff helps to support local artists, musicians, and performers.

Respect Local Customs And Traditions: Show respect for Bamberg's cultural heritage and traditions by adhering to local customs, etiquette, and clothing regulations. Learn about the city's history, customs, and traditions while interacting with inhabitants in a courteous and culturally aware manner.

In this chapter, we've looked at sustainable tourism practices in Bamberg, including as eco-friendly initiatives, responsible travel advice, and ways to help local communities. Visitors may help protect Bamberg's natural and cultural heritage for future generations by engaging in responsible travel practices and supporting sustainable tourism projects. Whether you're visiting the city's historic sites, dining at local eateries, or engaging in cultural activities, your choices as a responsible traveler may benefit the environment and the local community.

CHAPTER 20

LANGUAGE GUIDE

Whether you're a seasoned tourist or visiting Bamberg for the first time, knowing a few simple words in the local language will improve your experience and make it easier to communicate with locals. In this chapter, we'll present a complete reference to practical German words and expressions, with a focus on welcomes and introductions, ordering food and drinks, and asking for directions, so you may confidently and easily traverse the city.

Greetings And Introductions

Mastering basic greetings and introductions is essential for developing connection and making a good impression when engaging with Bamberg residents. Here are some key phrases to help you welcome people and start conversations:

Guten Morgen: Good morning

Guten Tag: Good day

Guten Abend: Good evening

Hallo: Hello

Wie Geht Es Ihnen?: How are you? (formal)

Wie Geht's?: How are you? (informal)

Ich Heiße...: My name is...

Wie Heißen Sie?: What is your name? (formal)

Wie Ist Ihr Name?: What is your name? (formal)

Wie Ist Dein Name?: What is your name? (informal)

Freut mich, Sie kennenzulernen: Nice to meet you (formal)

Freut Mich, Dich Kennenzulernen: Nice to meet you (informal)

Ordering Food And Drinks

Sampling local cuisine is a highlight of every trip to Bamberg, and learning how to order food and drinks in German can make your dining experience better. Here are some good phrases to use while eating out:

Eine Speisekarte, Bitte: A menu, please

Ich Hätte Gerne...: I would like...

Was Können Sie Empfehlen?: What do you recommend?

Haben Sie Vegetarische / Vegane Optionen?: Do you have vegetarian / vegan options?

Ich Hätte Gerne Das Tagesgericht: I'll have the daily special

Ein Tisch Für Zwei, Bitte: A table for two, please

Könnten Wir Die Rechnung Haben, Bitte?: Could we have the bill, please?

Ich Hätte Gerne Ein Bier / Glas Wein: I would like a beer / glass of wine

Welche Biere Haben Sie Vom Fass?: What draft beers do you have?

Ich Hätte Gerne Einen Kaffee, Bitte: I would like a coffee, please

Asking For Directions

Navigating Bamberg's streets can be an adventure in and of itself, but learning how to ask for directions in German will make it easier to find your way about. Here are some useful phrases you might use when asking for directions:

Entschuldigung, Können Sie Mir Helfen?: Excuse me, can you help me?

Wo Ist...?: Where is...?

Wie Komme Ich Zum...?: How do I get to the...?

Ist Es Weit Von Hier?: Is it far from here?

Gehen Sie Geradeaus / Links / Rechts: Go straight / left / right

Es Ist Um Die Ecke: It's around the corner

Entschuldigung, Ich habe Mich Verlaufen: Excuse me, I'm lost

Können Sie Mir Den Weg Zum Bahnhof Zeigen?: Can you show me the way to the train station?

Ich Suche Das Rathaus: I'm looking for the town hall

Können Sie Das Auf Der Karte Zeigen?: Can you show me on the map?

In this chapter, we've included a complete reference of important German phrases and expressions, with a focus on welcomes and introductions, ordering food and drinks, and getting directions. By learning these key phrases, you'll be able to confidently tour Bamberg, interact with people, and make the most of your time in this delightful city. Knowing a few simple words in German will improve your interactions and expand your cultural immersion in Bamberg, whether you're dining at local eateries, exploring historic buildings, or asking for directions to your next destination.

CHAPTER 21

FESTIVAL CALENDAR AND EVENTS GUIDE

Bamberg is noted for its strong cultural scene and year-round festivities. From traditional holidays to cultural and arts events, as well as sports and outdoor festivities, there is always something going on in Bamberg to keep inhabitants and visitors entertained. In this chapter, we'll look at the city's broad festival calendar and events guide, focusing on annual festivals and celebrations, cultural and artistic events, and sports and outdoor activities that display Bamberg's rich legacy and vibrant character.

Annual Festivals And Celebrations

Bamberg features a number of annual festivals and events that attract visitors from near and far. These events are deeply rooted in tradition and provide guests with an unparalleled opportunity to immerse themselves in Bamberg's rich cultural heritage. Here are some of the city's most important annual festivals and celebrations:

Sandkerwa: Held in August, Sandkerwa is Bamberg's largest and most famous event, bringing thousands of tourists to the city center. This week-long event includes live music, street performances, food stalls, and carnival rides, all culminating in a stunning fireworks show over the River Regnitz.

Bamberg Beer Festival (Bierkellerfest): Beer enthusiasts will not want to miss the annual Bamberg Beer Festival, which is hosted in several beer gardens and breweries throughout the city. This colorful festival celebrates Bamberg's famed brewing legacy, offering a diverse selection of local beers, traditional Bavarian cuisine, and live music entertainment.

Christmas Market (Weihnachtsmarkt): During the holiday season, Bamberg's picturesque old town is transformed into a winter wonderland with the annual Christmas Market. Visitors can peruse kiosks selling homemade crafts, Christmas decorations, and gastronomic delights while taking in the festive ambiance and seasonal music.

Easter Market (Ostermarkt): Every spring, Bamberg has an Easter Market in the city center, selling a variety of seasonal goods, artisanal products, and traditional Easter sweets. Visitors can buy for hand-painted eggs, wooden crafts, and local delicacies while listening to live music and watching cultural performances.

Franconian Beer Week (Fränkische Bierwoche): Beer lovers can enjoy a wide range of local brews during Franconian Beer Week, a 10-day celebration of Bavaria's brewing tradition. Throughout the week, participating breweries and beer gardens host special tastings, brewery tours, and beer-themed events.

Cultural And Arts Events

Bamberg's cultural calendar is packed with arts events such as music festivals, theater performances, and art exhibitions. Bamberg's dynamic cultural scene offers something for everyone, whether you prefer classical music, contemporary art, or traditional theater. Here are some of the city's best cultural and arts events:

Bamberg Jazz Festival: Every year, jazz fans rush to Bamberg for the annual Jazz Festival, which features local and international performers in various locations throughout the city. From intimate club performances to outdoor concerts in historic squares, the festival features a varied range of jazz styles and artists.

Bamberg International Film Festival: Film enthusiasts won't want to miss the Bamberg International Film Festival, a week-long celebration of world film. The festival includes independent cinema, documentary, and short film screenings, as well as panel discussions, director Q&A sessions, and special activities.

Bamberg Symphony Orchestra Concerts: Music fans can enjoy world-class performances by the Bamberg Symphony Orchestra, one of Germany's finest orchestras. The orchestra has a regular season of concerts in the Concert Hall Bamberg, which includes classical masterpieces, contemporary works, and guest performers from throughout the world.

Bamberg Art Walk (Bamberg Kunstspaziergang): Art lovers can discover Bamberg's lively art scene during the annual Art Walk, a city-wide event that showcases the work of local artists and galleries. Visitors can stroll through ancient streets and squares, stopping by participating sites to see exhibitions, hear artist presentations, and buy original artwork.

Bamberg Literature Festival (Bamberg Literaturfestival): Bookworms can indulge their love of literature at the Bamberg Literature Festival, an annual event that includes readings, author interviews, and literary debates. The festival brings together renowned authors, poets, and intellectuals to honor the written word and interact with readers.

Sports And Outdoor Festivals

Bamberg's attractive surroundings provide several options for outdoor recreation and sports throughout the year. From hiking and cycling to water sports and winter activities, Bamberg offers plenty of opportunities to get active and enjoy the great outdoors. Here are some of the city's most popular sports and outdoor festivities:

Regnitz River Rafting: Adventurers can enjoy the excitement of whitewater rafting on the Regnitz River, which runs through the heart of Bamberg. Guided rafting tours are available for all ability levels, and participants may navigate rapids while taking in stunning vistas of the city's historic buildings.

Bamberg Bicycle Tour: Cycling enthusiasts may discover Bamberg and its surrounds on a guided bicycle tour that takes them along scenic paths and gorgeous routes. Whether you enjoy relaxing rides through the countryside or strenuous mountain terrain, there is a cycling tour for everyone.

Bamberg City Run (Bamberg Stadtlauf): Fitness enthusiasts can lace up their running shoes and take part in the annual Bamberg City Run, a popular sporting event for runners of all ages and abilities. The race offers a variety of distances, ranging from a 5K fun run to a half marathon, allowing competitors to tour the city's sights on foot while enjoying the festive environment.

Winter Sports In The Fichtelgebirge Mountains: During the winter, outdoor enthusiasts can hit the slopes at the nearby Fichtelgebirge Mountains, where ski resorts provide skiing, snowboarding, and other winter sports activities. The region is a popular winter recreation destination, thanks to its magnificent alpine vistas and well-maintained routes.

Bamberg Dragon Boat Race: Paddler teams compete in the annual Bamberg Dragon Boat Race, an exciting water sports event conducted on the Regnitz River. Spectators can cheer on the colorful dragon boats as they race down the river, with live music, food stalls, and entertainment adding to the joyful vibe.

In this chapter, we looked at Bamberg's broad festival calendar and events guide, focusing on annual festivals and celebrations, cultural and arts events, and sports and outdoor activities that emphasize the city's lively cultural scene and dynamic attitude. Whether you prefer music, art, sports, or simply want to immerse yourself in local culture, Bamberg's busy festival schedule has something for everyone. From traditional Bavarian festivals to modern arts events, there's always something going on in Bamberg to entertain and inspire tourists all year.

CHAPTER 22

CONCLUSION

As your stay in Bamberg comes to an end, it's time to reflect on the unforgettable experiences you've had and say goodbye to this wonderful city. In this final chapter, we'll go over the highlights of your stay in Bamberg, provide some final suggestions and recommendations, and wish you safe travels as you continue your adventures.

Summary Of Highlights

During your time in Bamberg, you probably experienced numerous highlights and memorable events that left an indelible imprint. Some of the highlights of your time in Bamberg will include exploring the city's UNESCO World Heritage monuments and indulging in authentic Bavarian cuisine.

Exploring Bamberg's Old Town: Walk through the cobblestone streets of Bamberg's Old Town, taking in the breathtaking architecture and ancient buildings that have won the city UNESCO World Heritage status.

Sample Local Beer: Immerse yourself in Bamberg's brewing legacy by visiting traditional breweries and beer gardens across the city. Don't pass up the chance to enjoy Bamberg's famed smoked beer, a distinct and savory brew unlike anything you've ever tasted before.

Attending Festivals And Events: Get involved in Bamberg's rich cultural scene by visiting festivals, concerts, and events throughout the year. Whether you're celebrating at Sandkerwa, browsing the Christmas Market, or listening to live music during the Jazz Festival, there's always something spectacular going on in Bamberg.

Outdoor Activities: Take advantage of Bamberg's beautiful surroundings by going on hikes, cycling, and river cruises. Explore the picturesque pathways of the Franconian countryside, or take a leisurely boat trip along the River Regnitz for a unique view of the city.

Indulge In Culinary Delights: Sample the flavors of Franconian cuisine in local restaurants and eateries throughout Bamberg. From meaty sausages and schnitzels to savory pretzels and sumptuous desserts, you'll find plenty of tasty options to quench your hunger.

Final Tips And Recommendations

As you prepare to leave Bamberg and continue your journey, here are some final suggestions and recommendations to guarantee a smooth and pleasurable trip:

Pack Lightly: When preparing for your trip, remember to carry only the necessities. Bamberg's modest size allows you to explore on foot, so you'll welcome having less luggage to carry while you navigate the city's streets and sights.

Learn Basic German Phrases: Brush up on your German language abilities before arriving in Bamberg, as knowing a few basic words will improve your experience and allow you to communicate with locals more successfully.

Respect Local Customs And Etiquette: Learn about local customs and etiquette in Bamberg to ensure that you respect the city's cultural heritage and traditions. From greeting residents with a cheerful "Guten Tag" to maintaining table manners when dining out, respecting local customs will enhance your cultural immersion experience.

Be Flexible And Open-Minded: As you explore Bamberg, embrace spontaneity and have an open mind, because some of the best experiences frequently happen when you least expect them. Allow yourself to walk off the beaten route and find hidden jewels that may not be listed in guidebooks.

Capture Memories: Don't forget to document your time in Bamberg with photos, movies, and journals. These artifacts will serve as permanent reminders of your adventures, allowing you to relive them long after you've returned home.

Wishing You Safe Travels

As you leave Bamberg and embark on your next adventure, we give our best wishes for safe travels and great experiences. May your memories of Bamberg last a lifetime, and may you continue to explore the globe with curiosity, wonder, and adventure.

In this final chapter, we've reviewed the highlights of your stay in Bamberg, provided some final suggestions and recommendations, and wished you safe travels as you continue your journey. Whether you're leaving Bamberg with fond memories or planning a return visit, we hope your time here has made an indelible imprint and motivated you to explore new places with passion and excitement. Farewell till we meet again, and may your travels bring you joy, exploration, and adventure.

CHAPTER 23

APPENDIX

This appendix contains a variety of valuable materials to help you get the most out of your visit to Bamberg, Germany. These resources, which range from emergency contacts to navigational tools and additional reading materials, will help you confidently traverse the city and make the most of your visit in this delightful destination.

Emergency Contacts

When visiting a new place, it's crucial to be prepared for any unexpected events. Here are some emergency contacts to keep ready while you are in Bamberg:

Emergency Services: In the event of an emergency, phone 112 for quick assistance from police, fire, or ambulance.

Bamberg Police Department: For non-emergency police help, call +49 951 9129-0.

Bamberg Fire Department: For fire situations, dial 112 or call +49 951 19449.

Medical Emergencies: Call 112 or go to the nearest hospital or clinic.

Maps And Navigation Tools

Maps and navigational tools make it easier to navigate Bamberg's streets. Here are some resources to help you find your way around the city.

Google Maps (www.maps.google.com): Available on desktop and mobile devices, Google Maps offers detailed maps, directions, and navigation services for exploring Bamberg and its surroundings.

Bamberg City Map (www.bamberg.de/en): Go to the city of Bamberg's official website to download or view a printable city map that highlights significant attractions, landmarks, and sites of interest.

Additional Reading And References

For further knowledge and insights on Bamberg's history, culture, and attractions, examine these supplementary reading materials and references:

"Bamberg: UNESCO World Heritage City" By Hans-Jürgen Schierschmidt: This thorough guidebook provides an in-depth investigation of Bamberg's UNESCO World Heritage monuments, including historical context, architectural details, and insider information for tourists.

"Bamberg: A Cultural Guide" By Klaus Gallas: With this comprehensive guidebook, you may discover Bamberg's cultural riches, including museums, galleries, theaters, and festivals.

"Bamberg Beer Guide" By Michael Jackson: Beer fans will enjoy this guide to Bamberg's famed brewing legacy, which includes profiles of local breweries, tasting notes, and beer-related activities.

Useful Local Phrases

Communicating with locals in their original language can improve your travel experience and establish lasting relationships. Here are some essential local terms that will assist you navigate conversations in Bamberg.

"Guten Tag": Good day

"Bitte": Please

"Danke": Thank you

"Entschuldigung": Excuse me

"Sprechen Sie Englisch?": Do you speak English?

"Wo Ist...?": Where is...?

"Ich Hätte Gerne...": I would like...

"Wie Viel Kostet Das?": How much does this cost?

Familiarizing yourself with these simple phrases can help you communicate with locals and manage everyday circumstances more easily during your stay in Bamberg..

In this appendix, we've provided a selection of useful resources to enhance your experience in Bamberg, Germany. From emergency contacts to navigational tools and additional reading materials, these resources will help you make the most of your visit and ensure a memorable and enjoyable stay in this charming city. Whether you're seeking emergency assistance, navigating the streets, or delving into Bamberg's rich history and culture, these resources will serve as valuable tools to enhance your travel experience.

Addresses And Locations Of Popular Accommodation

When organizing your trip in Bamberg, it is critical to select accommodations that meet your needs and budget. Below is a list of popular hotels, guesthouses, and other lodging alternatives, along with their addresses and locations:

Welcome Hotel Residenzschloss Bamberg

Address: Untere Sandstraße 32, 96049 Bamberg, Germany.

Website: www.welcome-hotels.com/hotels/bamberg

Hotel Nepomuk

Address: Obere Mühlbrücke 9-11, 96049 Bamberg, Germany.

Website: www.hotel-nepomuk.de/en/

Altstadt-Hotel Molitor

Address: Obere Mühlbrücke 9-11, 96049 Bamberg, Germany.

Website: www.molitor-bamberg.de/en/

Hotel Villa Geyersvörth

Address: Geyersvörthstraße 5, 96047 Bamberg, Germany.

Website: www.villa-geyersvoerth.de/en/

Am Blumenhaus

Address: Untere Sandstraße 16, 96049 Bamberg, Germany.

Website: www.am-blumenhaus.de/en/

Addresses And Locations Of Popular Restaurants And Cafés

Bamberg is well-known for its culinary scene, which offers a diverse choice of dining alternatives to satisfy all tastes. Here are several popular restaurants and cafés, including their addresses and locations:

Schlenkerla Brewery Tavern

Address: Dominikanerstraße 6, 96049 Bamberg, Germany.

Website: www.schlenkerla.de/

Spezial-Keller

Address: Obere Königstraße 10, 96052 Bamberg, Germany.

Website: www.spezial-keller.de/

Gasthaus Wilde Rose

Address: Lange Straße 41, 96047 Bamberg, Germany.

Website: www.wilderose-bamberg.de/

Café Müller

Address: Oberer Stephansberg 7, 96049 Bamberg, Germany.

Website: www.cafe-mueller-bamberg.de/

Fässla Brewery

Address: Obere Königstraße 19, 96052 Bamberg, Germany.

Website: www.faessla.de/

Addresses And Locations Of Popular Bars And Clubs

There are numerous bars and clubs in Bamberg for those wishing to experience the city's nightlife. Listed below are several popular venues, along with their addresses and locations:

Schlenkerla Brewery Tavern

Address: Dominikanerstraße 6, 96049 Bamberg, Germany.

Website: www.schlenkerla.de/

Live-Club Bamberg

Address: Pödeldorfer Straße 60, 96052 Bamberg, Germany.

Website: www.live-club.de/

Stilbruch

Address: Obere Sandstraße 6, 96049 Bamberg, Germany.

Website: www.stilbruch-bamberg.de/

Pillhofer Bar And Café

Address: Obere Sandstraße 17, 96049 Bamberg, Germany.

Website: www.pillhofer-bar.de/

Kapitel 12

Address: Kapitelstraße 12, 96047 Bamberg, Germany.

Website: www.kapitel12.de/

Addresses And Locations Of Top Attractions

Bamberg has a multitude of historical landmarks, cultural attractions, and scenic views to see. Here are the addresses and locations of some of the city's most popular attractions:

Bamberg Cathedral (Bamberger Dom)

Address: Domplatz 2, 96049 Bamberg, Germany.

Old Town Hall (Altes Rathaus)

Address: Obere Brücke, 96047 Bamberg, Germany.

New Residence (Neue Residenz)

Address: Domplatz 8, 96049 Bamberg, Germany.

Altenburg Castle (Schloss Altenburg)

Address: Altenburg 1, 96049 Bamberg, Germany.

Little Venice (Klein-Venedig)

Address: Untere Sandstraße, 96049 Bamberg, Germany.

Using the addresses and locations listed above, you may easily find popular lodging options, dining places, nightlife venues, and must-see attractions during your trip to Bamberg.

This appendix contains addresses and locations for popular accommodations, restaurants, cafés, pubs, clubs, and top attractions in Bamberg, Germany. Whether you're looking for a place to stay, eat, or explore, this thorough guide will help you plan your itinerary and traverse the city easily. Make the most of your time in Bamberg by visiting these notable places and discovering the finest that the city has to offer.

MAPS

Map Of Bamberg

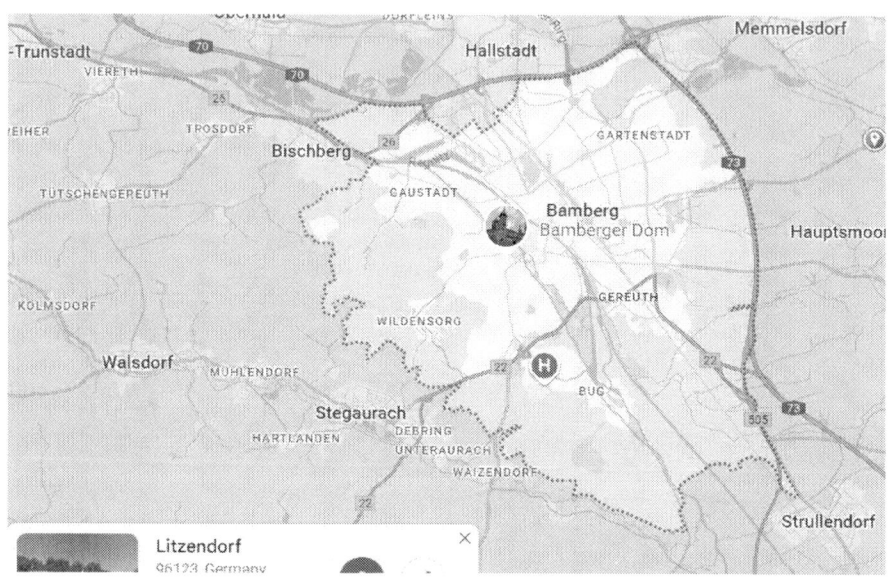

https://maps.app.goo.gl/ySQ2MDppTAkCP3jA7

**USE YOUR PHONE TO SCAN THE QR
CODE IMAGE TO GET THE LOCATIONS
IN REAL TIME**

Things To Do In Bamberg

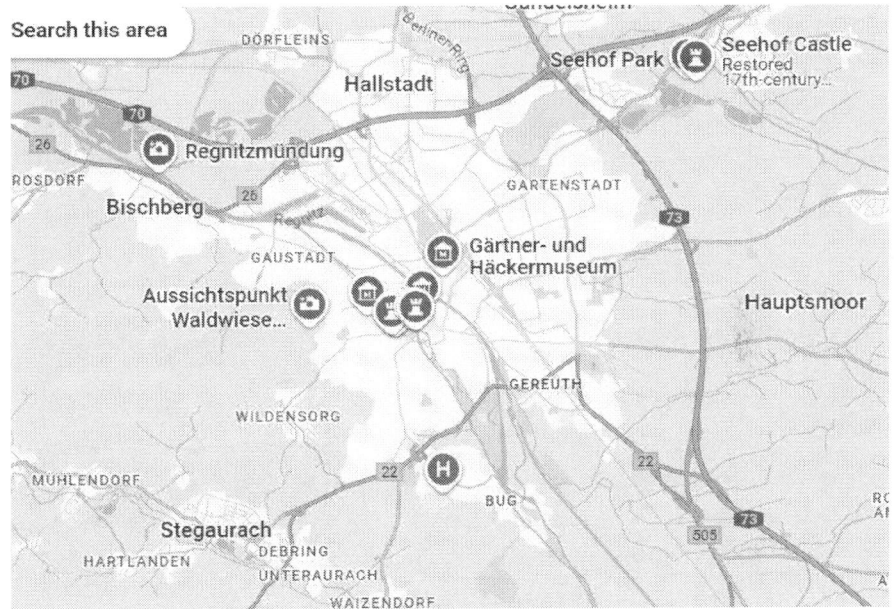

https://maps.app.goo.gl/uo2HWL8g1h4ZfcKy8

USE YOUR PHONE TO SCAN THE QR
CODE IMAGE TO GET THE LOCATIONS
IN REAL TIME

Hotels In Bamberg

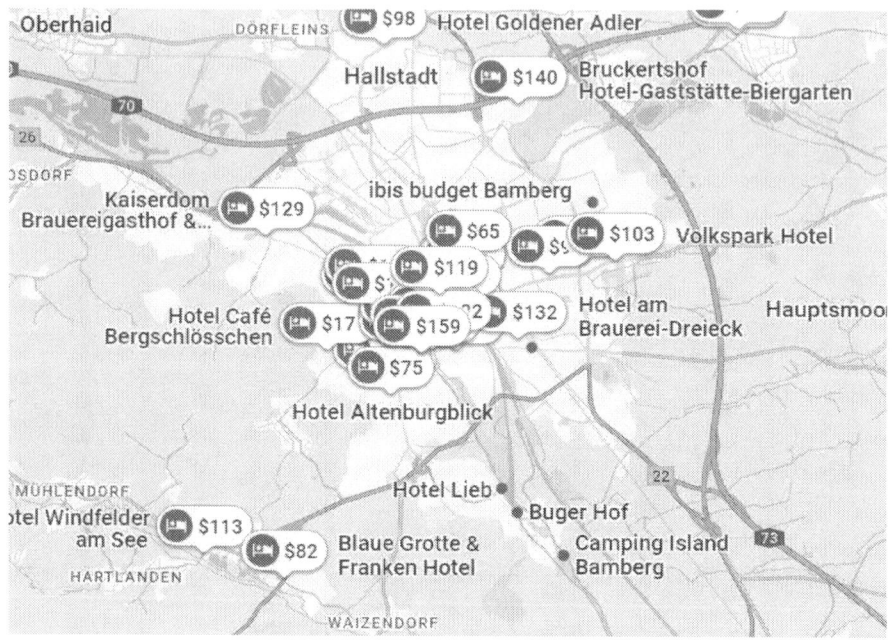

https://maps.app.goo.gl/cWphPrwnZJRHcLQu9

USE YOUR PHONE TO SCAN THE QR CODE IMAGE TO GET THE LOCATIONS IN REAL TIME

Vacation Rentals In Bamberg

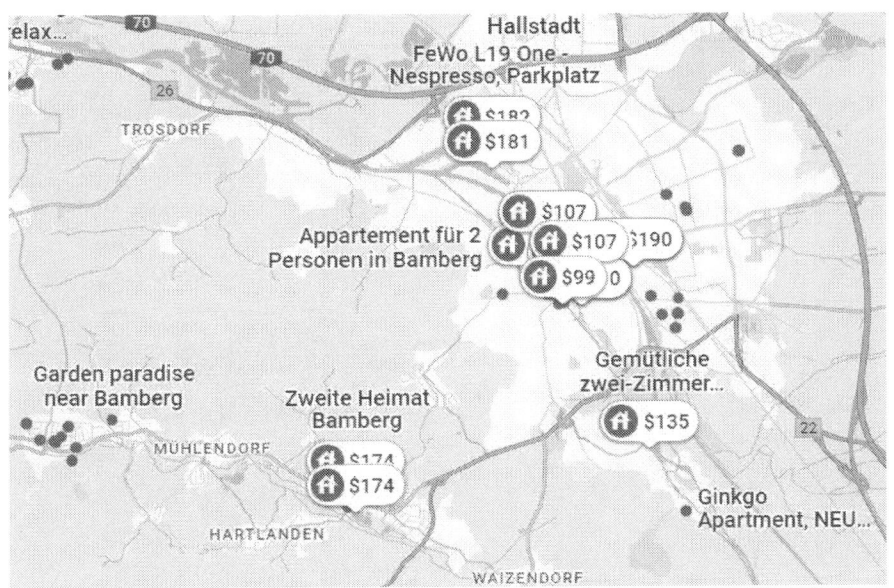

https://maps.app.goo.gl/DqWyRQFgFpQniokw5

USE YOUR PHONE TO SCAN THE QR CODE IMAGE TO GET THE LOCATIONS IN REAL TIME

Restaurants In Bamberg

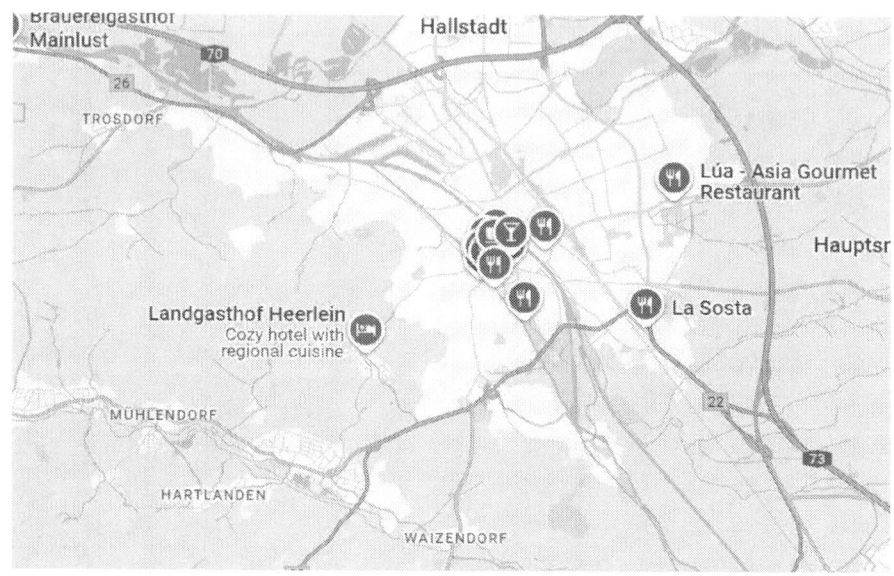

https://maps.app.goo.gl/otd64qpPDX1Q4Ner6

USE YOUR PHONE TO SCAN THE QR CODE IMAGE TO GET THE LOCATIONS IN REAL TIME

Museums In Bamberg

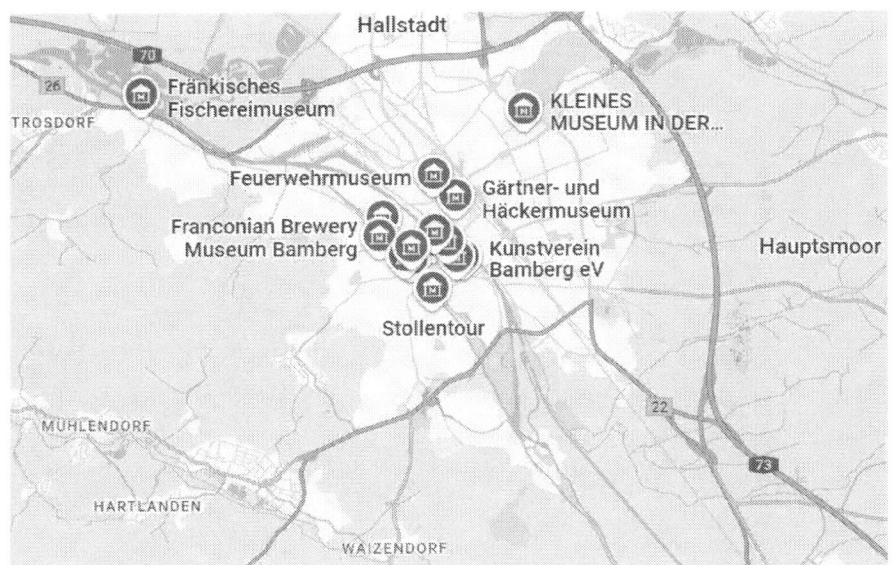

https://maps.app.goo.gl/YNjKemR2HaWqKXVA9

USE YOUR PHONE TO SCAN THE QR CODE IMAGE TO GET THE LOCATIONS IN REAL TIME

Transit Stations In Bamberg

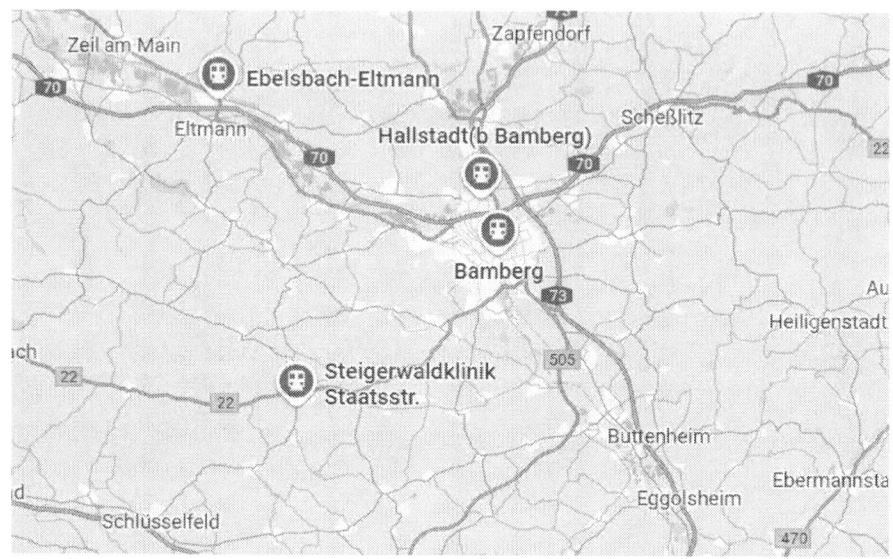

https://maps.app.goo.gl/xZ1GNzarXj2gFGGu5

**USE YOUR PHONE TO SCAN THE QR
CODE IMAGE TO GET THE
LOCATIONS IN REAL TIME**

Pharmacies In Bamberg

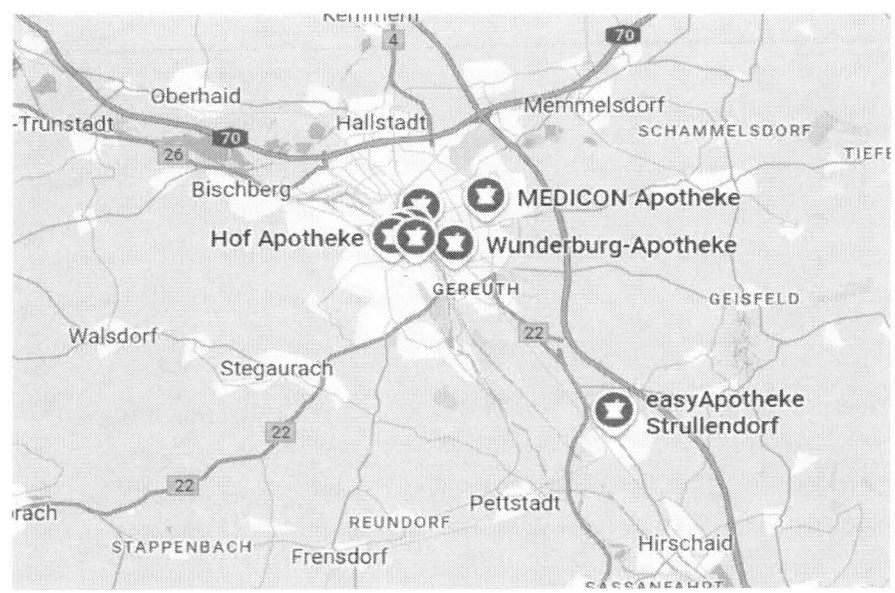

https://maps.app.goo.gl/HTPWmTrhSZoijseJ9

USE YOUR PHONE TO SCAN THE QR CODE IMAGE TO GET THE LOCATIONS IN REAL TIME

ATMs In Bamberg

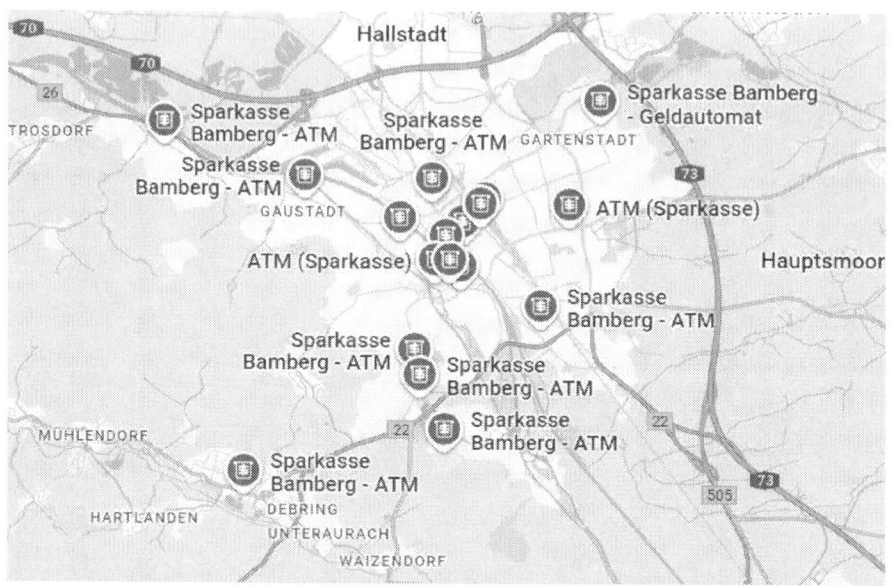

https://maps.app.goo.gl/efXXsdEDo8cXTvbR6

USE YOUR PHONE TO SCAN THE QR CODE IMAGE TO GET THE LOCATIONS IN REAL TIME

Hiking Trails In Bamberg

https://maps.app.goo.gl/ctHjPXq9hPfX2Q5k6

**USE YOUR PHONE TO SCAN THE QR
CODE IMAGE TO GET THE LOCATIONS
IN REAL TIME**

IMAGE ATTRIBUTION

APPRECIATION

Thank you so much for purchasing **Kiera Clayton's Travel Guide**! I truly appreciate your support and hope this guide helps you create amazing memories on your journey. Your feedback means the world to me, so if you found this book helpful, I would love it if you could take a moment to leave a review. Your thoughts not only help me improve, but also assist other travelers in planning their perfect trip. Thank you again, and happy travels!

Made in United States
Troutdale, OR
02/03/2025

28605843R00124